The nature and work of plants; an introduction to the study of botany

Daniel Trembly Macdougal

THE NATURE AND WORK
OF PLANTS

The Co

THE NATURE AND WORK
OF PLANTS

An Introduction to the Study of Botany

BY

DANIEL TREMBLY MACDOUGAL, Ph.D.

DIRECTOR OF THE LABORATORIES, NEW YORK
BOTANICAL GARDEN

New York

THE MACMILLAN COMPANY

LONDON: MACMILLAN & CO., Ltd.

1900

Norwood Press
J. S. Cushing & Co — Berwick & Smith
Norwood Mass U S A.

PREFACE

THE course outlined in this little book is essentially a study of the functions or action of the plant, and organs are considered chiefly as instruments for the performance of work, with but little attention to their morphology. It is believed that this method of introduction to the subject of botany will be best suited for beginners who have not at hand the facilities of a laboratory. In conformity with this idea, the use of technical terms has been restricted to the actual necessities of logical treatment, and the demonstrations have been developed by the simplest experimental methods.

Material. — The apparatus needed to carry out the work may be found in any household, with the exception of the hand lens, which may be purchased for less than a dollar; a glass which will magnify six to ten times will be sufficient. A supply of plant material is, of course, indispensable. Students having access to greenhouses will be able to secure specimens to illustrate the entire course without difficulty. If the plants of the woods and fields are to be used, as many observations as possible should be carried out in the summer, spring, and autumn, and a supply of roots, corms, tubers, bulbs, seeds, and fruits, should be collected for use during the winter season. Many of these may be preserved in the same manner as potatoes, and forced to grow when brought into a warm living-room in January or later. This may be done with the material used in the following paragraphs: 8, 10, 13, 19, 26, 38, 39, 43, 44, 45, 46, 47, 48, 50, 51, 53, 54, 77, 97, 106, 108, 109, 120, 129, 148, 165, 167, 168, 169, 180, 181, 182, 183, 184, 185, 195, 211, 212, 213, 214, 216, 217, 225, and 229.

Desirable material may be obtained from dealers in native plants if the student is unable to collect it himself. It is quite important that the plants used should be properly identified, and this may be done by the use of a manual of the flora of the region in which the work is done, which may be selected from the following list:—

Britton and Brown, Flora of the Northern States and Canada, Charles Scribner's Sons, New York.

GRAY, Manual of Botany, American Book Company, New York City.

CHAPMAN, Flora of the Southern States, Cambridge Botanical Supply Company, Cambridge, Mass.

COULTER, Flora of Western Texas, United States Department of Agriculture, Washington, D. C.

GREENE, Manual of Botany of the Region of San Francisco Bay, Cubery & Co., San Francisco.

HOWELL, Flora of Northwest America.

COULTER, Manual of Rocky Mountain Botany, American Book Company, New York City

GRAY, Field, Forest, and Garden Botany, American Book Company, New York City.

It will also be found profitable to read the discussions of the various subjects in the following works, which may also suggest further lines of experimentation . —

KERNER and OLIVER, Natural History of Plants, Holt & Co., New York City.

COULTER, Plant Relations, D Appleton & Co , New York City.

BARNES, Plant Life, Holt & Co , New York City

BAILEY, Lessons with Plants, Macmillan Company, New York City

ATKINSON, Elementary Botany, Holt & Co., New York City.

MacDOUGAL, Experimental Plant Physiology, Holt & Co , New York City.

ARTHUR and MacDOUGAL, Living Plants and their Properties, Morris & Wilson, Minneapolis.

The author acknowledges substantial aid from Professor Francis E. Lloyd in the revision of the manuscript and the reading of proof, and many valuable suggestions from Mrs. E. G. Britton.

D. T. McD.

NEW YORK BOTANICAL GARDEN,
January, 1900.

CONTENTS

I. THE COMPOSITION AND PURPOSES OF PLANTS

II. THE MATERIAL OF WHICH PLANTS ARE MADE UP

III THE MANNER IN WHICH DIFFERENT KINDS OF WORK ARE DIVIDED AMONG THE MEMBERS OF THE BODY

V. THE LEAVES

VI. STEMS

VII   The Way in which New Plants Arise

VIII. SEEDS AND FRUITS

IX. The Power or Energy of the Plant

X. Relations of Plants to Each Other, and the Place in which they Live

THE NATURE AND WORK OF PLANTS

I. THE COMPOSITION AND PURPOSES OF PLANTS

1. *The plant is composed of living matter.* — The tints of a flower, the graceful curves of a twining vine, and the uncouth forms of the cactus claim our attention, because they excite our curiosity and admiration. These and many other features of the vegetable world become of much greater interest, however, when it is learned that the color of the rose, the lacelike fronds of the fern, the imposing trunk of the forest tree, the spines of the thistle, and the juicy sweetness of a berry are all due to the action of a wonderful substance, which is known to be living, and is usually termed *protoplasm*. If our studies are extended, we may learn that this living substance is the most important part of our bodies, as well as those of all other animals and of

B   1

plants also.   Still further it would be found that protoplasm has certain ways of doing things, certain modes of action, or is governed by a number of laws, no matter whether it is in the body of a plant or animal.   Very little is known of the composition of protoplasm, except that a great many kinds of material are used in its construction, and that these materials are blended and woven together in a very complex and intricate manner.   Protoplasm is a very delicate and sensitive substance, easily destroyed or injured, hence when it forms the body of a plant or animal, it is generally necessary for it to construct masses or sheets of lifeless substance, which it fashions into tools for the performance of its work, or into coverings which hide it from sight and protect its fragile mechanism from damage by heat, cold, dryness, or other agencies which might crush, tear, or injure it in any manner.   The yellowish masses of slimy substance to be seen on decaying logs are the bodies of a slime mould which is composed of naked protoplasm.   This organism is so low in the scale of life that it is difficult to say whether it is more like a plant or an animal, and it forms coverings for its protoplasm in the reproductive stage only.

2. *The purposes of plants.* — The chief purpose
of every individual plant is to give rise to other
individuals of the same kind. In carrying out this
purpose the protoplasm strives constantly to perfect
itself, or rather its tools and organs, and to adapt
these more exactly to the conditions of light, moisture, temperature, and the food supply under which
it is compelled to live. The manner in which the
living substance attempts to improve its own mechanism and the usefulness of its tools determines the
form and structure of its body, and accounts largely
for the differences between an oak tree and a violet.

3. *Great differences among plants.* — It needs but
the most casual glance at a field or forest to find
that there are many different kinds of plants in
it. Thus it is easily seen that some are grasses forming a thick velvety carpet of sod on the surface of
the soil, while others are trees and send their round
trunks a hundred feet into the air. The differences
between the grasses and the trees are very great, but
all plants are not so much unlike as these two groups.
It will be found that there are many kinds of trees
and many kinds of grasses. Thus to one familiar
with the out-of-door world, the maple tree is not to

be confused with the oak or beech, or the walnut with the sycamore, while the pine and poplar are so unlike that they might be distinguished even at night. In the same manner the mosses and ferns comprise many forms. The simple plants which float upon the surface of the water in ponds also show various colors, shapes, and methods of forming colonies in evidence that they do not all live alike.

4. *The oaks, maples, elms, ferns, mosses, and pond scums are not all of the same kind among themselves.* — Now if one goes through a forest and looks carefully at all of the maple trees he may see in a half day's walk, he will find that they do not all have the same appearance.

In the Middle states one is very likely to see " sugar maples " (*Acer saccharum*), large handsome trees, over a hundred feet high, many of them with grayish bark, large leaves, flowers greenish-yellow in color, appearing at the same time as the leaves, and the trunk is very full of a sweetish sap in the spring. On the edges of swamps and in the low grounds will be found other maple trees, with the bark of the twigs quite reddish in color, leaves with sharp-pointed lobes and some hairs on the veins, the flowers yellowish-red, and appearing before the leaves in the spring. The leaves show the most brilliant colors in the autumn. This is the red maple (*Acer rubrum*), and the sugar maple and the red maple trees each constitute a species. The trees of each species live in certain kinds of places, and have distinct forms of leaves, twigs, fruit, and flowers adapted to the conditions under which they exist, and these organs are developed at such season in the two species as will enable each to do its work in the best manner.

The violets are among the earliest spring flowers, and it would be possible in a great many localities to find some with white, others with blue, and others with yellow flowers. Dig up a specimen of each and lay them side by side on the table or a sheet of paper. Compare the roots, stems, leaves, and flowers, as to their number, where attached, form, and color.

This will show that the three violets have developed their organs in various manners, and that the three are members of three different species of the violets.

A good conception of the difference between species may be gained from a comparison of a wild cherry tree with those in any orchard, and of the slippery elm with the white elm.

5. *A species.* — In an examination of a number of sugar maple or red maple trees it will be seen that they are not all exactly the same size, shape, and color, but that the red maples show some differences among themselves. In the same manner the violets with yellow flowers are not exactly the same shape and size as to leaves and stems. Still the yellow violet plants are more like each other than they are like the blue violets.

We are now ready to define a species, and can say that a species is a group of individuals very much alike one another, but unlike the individuals of another species. Further, if the seeds of the yellow violet are planted, they will germinate and form plants which are like those from which the seeds were taken. It may then be said that the seeds of any species reproduce or give rise to the same kind of specimens as those which bore the seed. The seeds of blue violets always produce blue violets, those of yellow violets always produce yellow violets, and so on through the whole list of over a hundred thousand species of plants which form seeds. The groups of individuals which represent the species may alter their habits and general appearance, little by little, from generation to generation, until in the course of

a great many years individuals are produced quite
unlike the originals; yet there are no abrupt changes
or jumps from one form to another. Thus, for instance, the belief, quite common in some farming
communities, that wheat can be converted into
"Chess," or "Cheat," is founded on an utter impos-
sibility. It will be shown later (§ 197) that plants
have two generations, or two forms which alternate
with each other, and these two forms are quite
prominent in the mosses; but in such cases the two
forms are equally invariable and may not be changed
quickly or suddenly.

The chief point of interest in the idea of a species
in connection with the work to be followed in this
book is the fact that a species is a group of individuals that are trying to adapt themselves to a certain
mode of life by means of the special organs in the
forms of stems, leaves, roots, and flowers in the
higher plants, and by organs which do the same
work among the lower forms. And furthermore,
that no two species try to live in exactly the same
manner.

6. *Scope of work described.* — The studies described in the following pages make up an outline

of examination of the plant at work, and consist of observations on the structure of the organs of the plant machine, the things which the plant may do, the way in which it secures food, avoids injury, and accomplishes reproduction.

An attempt will be made to determine not only the kinds of work a plant may do, but in some instances the opportunity will be taken to measure the amount it may accomplish in the same manner that the capacity of an engine might be noted.

II. THE MATERIAL OF WHICH PLANTS ARE MADE UP

7. *The plant is an engine.* — The plant is a machine, and is composed of many more separate parts than a watch or locomotive. The construction of a watch or locomotive may be learned by tearing one to pieces, or by building it up from its separate parts. After this has been done it is much easier to understand the action of these machines. The same is true of the plant.

The composition of the plant might be found by separating it into its different substances, after the manner of the chemist, or by building it up from the materials of which it may be composed. Neither of these methods is entirely satisfactory when used alone, because they cannot be completely carried out. The substances or compounds in protoplasm are so delicate that when we seek to separate them they are destroyed. The result is the same as if we attempted to tear down a building made of bricks so fragile that they would crumble at the touch;

when we have finished we have nothing but a pile of rubbish and dust.

Then, again, we cannot actually construct protoplasm with our own hands; but we may ascertain the substances which should be given to the protoplasm of a plant in the form of food, in order that it should be able to grow or add to its bulk. While both of these methods are subject to so many errors that they are but of little use separately, yet both together give a fair knowledge of the composition of the bodies of plants.

8. *Water, charcoal, and ash.* — Place enough freshly gathered leaves or stems to make about half a pound in a small tin dish, and set on the pan of a balance. Weigh carefully. Now place the pan on the top of a stove for two or three hours, or in the hot sunlight for twice that time. Weigh again. How much weight has been lost? Set fire to the dried material and attend to it until it is completely burned, being careful that none of the ash is allowed to escape from the dish. Now weigh again. How much weight has been lost this time? Clean out the pan and weigh. Subtract the weight of the dish from the figures obtained at each weighing and you

will have first the weight of the fresh material, about half a pound. When the fresh plant is dried, it needs no demonstration to show that water is driven off, so that the next weight represents the material in the plant after the water is taken away. This dried material is composed of two different kinds of substances. When it is burned, one kind, constituting the charcoal, is consumed, leaving only the ash or mineral substances behind. If these weighings are carefully made, it will be found that the water makes more than three-fourths of a growing plant, the charcoal generally less than one-fourth, and the ash only one-fortieth or one-fiftieth of the total weight. The ashes that collect in a stove are exactly similar to those obtained in this experiment, of course; and it is well known that the weight of the ash from a heavy armful of wood is very small. This experiment may also be carried out with a potato, carrot, or turnip.

The relative amounts of the different groups of substances vary with the species of plants examined and the age of the specimens. The greatest proportion of water is to be found in young shoots, the greatest proportion of charcoal in old woody stems, and the greatest proportion of ash in leaves.

This last fact is due to the action of the current of water which constantly travels upward through the stem into the leaves where it evaporates and passes off into the air, leaving behind all the mineral substance brought up from the soil.

9. *Leaves shrink in drying.* — During the drying process the loss of water brings the particles of which the plant is composed closer together, and it shrinks in size. This may be best seen in leaves. Place a leaf of sunflower or some fresh rapidly growing leaf on a sheet of paper, and trace its outline with a pencil. Now put it between two sheets of blotting paper on which is placed a weight of ten pounds. Replace the blotting paper twice a day for three or four days. Place the dried leaf over the original tracing, and make a second drawing of its outline. The leaf has decreased in length and width. Measure the amount.

10. *Mineral coatings.* — During the life of the plant the mineral substances in it are usually dissolved in water and are not visible. In some instances, however, these minerals take the form of small crystals which can be seen with the microscope. In still other cases the mineral is deposited

on the outside of the plant as a hard covering easily visible. This is especially true of the scouring rush (*Equisetum*). A complete coat of *silicon* covers the surface of the stem and gives a rough feeling when handled. The mineral sheath is so heavy that the tissues of the plant may be destroyed and it will remain intact. To demonstrate this, put two or three short pieces of the stem of the scouring rush into a dish or test tube and cover with a mixture of three parts water and one part *hydrochloric acid* (*muriatic acid*) Warm the preparation nearly to the boiling point for two hours. Pour off the acid and wash with clean water two or three times. The beautiful silicon sheath may now be handled and preserved in water indefinitely.

The silicon sheath may be separated in a still more simple manner if a section of the stem is held in the blaze of a fire or the flame of a lamp. The water will be driven off, the dried material will burn, and then the mineral sheath will reach a red heat, retaining its original shape. This may be preserved dry or in water.

11. *Uses of mineral coatings* — The mineral covering of the scouring rush prevents grazing animals

from biting the stems, although it is not known whether they were formed for that purpose or not. In some instances mineral substances are deposited on the bodies of plants in the same way in which they are accumulated on the bottom of a kettle in which water is boiled, and are not only of no use to the plant, but are a detriment to growth and food formation.

Certain species living in localities where there is but little rainfall and where the air is very dry, however, have a layer of salts on the surfaces of the leaves, which attracts water from the air, thus preventing these useful organs from drying out. The mineral coating of a stem may also serve a similar purpose.

12. *Aquatic species with mineral coatings.* — Many plants which live in the water cause the mineral matter dissolved in it to be deposited on their surfaces. This may be seen on the pond weeds (*Potamogetons*), if specimens are taken from the water and allowed to dry. Some of the small threadlike algæ are said to be "calcareous" because they are found surrounded by masses of lime of greater bulk than their own bodies. Many of the

curious rock formations in the Yellowstone Park are made up in this manner. Some of the powders used to polish metals are taken from deposits in the soil, and they consist of the silicon sheath of minute plants.

13. *"Water cultures" with and without mineral salts.* — Fill a quart fruit jar with clean rain water, and a second from a stream or pond. Put in each a freshly cut twig of willow (*Salix*) or a stem of coleus, and place both in sunlight in a warm room. Replace the water weekly, and clean out the jars. The cuttings will soon begin to grow and form leaves, even if the experiment is performed in winter. Compare the amount of growth in three or four weeks. Have they grown equally? If a difference is shown in the number and size of the leaves and roots, to what is it due? The following demonstration may throw some light on the subject.

14. *Ash or mineral salts in the water of streams.* — Boil a quart of rain water in a dish with a polished inner surface until the liquid has all disappeared. Examine the bottom of the dish. Nothing has been left behind, and rain water is seen to be

lacking in solid matter which might be used as food by the plant.

Now boil a quart of water from a stream or pond in the same dish until it has all passed away in the form of vapor. A gray coating remains on the bottom of the dish, consisting of mineral salts, which may be taken up by the plant, and which forms the ash when it is burned. This is identical with the "lime" which is deposited on the inside of tea-kettles in which hard water is boiled.

15. *Elements found in plants.* — If a complete chemical analysis were made of the plant, it would be found that it had selected *sulphur, phosphorus, magnesium, calcium, potassium, sodium,* and *iron* from the minerals present and had taken these up in certain proportions most useful to it. Besides these, it also gets *nitrogen, chlorine, carbon, hydrogen,* and *oxygen* from the soil and air. Many species take up quantities of *silicon,* as did the scouring rush. The seaweeds use *iodine* and *bromine,* and still other elements are taken up by a few forms, and may or may not serve as food. Thus many of the grasses and sedges do this, and some of them use the mineral to give a sharp saw-toothed edge to their

leaves, which cut like knives when drawn care-lessly through the hand. This device may well be a protection against animals, for they will not only not eat such plants, but avoid walking among them.

The plant may pick up almost any salt in the soil penetrated by its roots, of even such poisonous substances as *zinc, antimony, arsenic,* or *copper*. The wood of large numbers of trees growing in the regions which have copper-bearing rock in the soil may contain as much as one per cent of their dry weight in copper, although this metal is of no use to the plant and is slightly poisonous to it. The same is true in regard to zinc and arsenic. In general, it may be said that no substance is taken up in great proportion unless used as food.

Animals, especially man, take in substances in food which do not actually enter into the tissues of the body, but promote the digestion and use of the necessary elements. The same will apply in some degree to plants. It is necessary for the proper absorption and use of the indispensable food substances that others should be present with them which are not used. Thus the plant does not use *sodium* in constructing protoplasm, yet it should have this substance in its food solutions.

c

16. *Substances serving as food.* — A fairly perfect food for the plants in the water culture experiment described in § 13 may be made by adding to each quart of rain water put into the jars ten grains each of *common salt, plaster of Paris, Epsom salts, calcium phosphate,* and a few drops of *iron chloride.* It will be noted that common salt is a compound of *sodium* and *chlorine.* The sodium does not actually enter into the body of the plant, yet its presence in the food is quite useful.

17. *Compounds in the plants.* — The different substances taken up by the plant consist of twelve or thirteen elements, and these are united again in such manner as to form many hundreds of different compounds. The formation of these compounds is generally for some specific purpose. Thus *sugar* is built up from the *carbon, hydrogen,* and *oxygen* taken from the food substances, and it is used in the construction of living matter, kept as a reserve material, or it may be sent from one part of the body of the plant to another. *Acids* are formed for many purposes, *cellulose* for cell walls and coverings for the protoplasm, *proteins* to build up the living substance itself, which is constantly wearing out.

18. *Tests for the contents of the plant.* — If a raw potato is crushed in clear water, the latter becomes milky, and by placing some of it in a small glass and holding up to the window, numbers of minute granules may be seen. They are not more than a hundredth of an inch in diameter. If a few drops of a tincture of *iodine* obtained from a druggist is added to the water, it turns blue, owing to the action of iodine upon *starch*. Put a drop of the tincture on the cut surface of the potato and note the result.

Apply iodine to the cut surfaces of stems and roots, and determine the portions in which starch may be found.

Sugar in sugar-cane, sorghum, fruits, or the sugar beet, or in the sap of the maple, may be detected by the taste, and the sour acids may be found in the same manner.

If you were to take the plant to a chemical laboratory, and make a complete chemical analysis of it, a large number of other substances would be found, such as *oils, tannins, alkaloids, proteins, mineral salts*, etc.

Animals, including man, have found uses for many of these substances, and species which produce them are grown or cultivated in great numbers. It is to be borne in mind that the species was not developed for the purpose of being useful to anything except itself. Man has learned to take advantage of the capacity of the plant for forming certain substances, and cultivates these species in order to get their products. This intelligent action is shared by certain lower animals which cultivate crops of moulds and use them for food.

III. THE MANNER IN WHICH DIFFERENT KINDS OF WORK ARE DIVIDED AMONG THE MEMBERS OF THE BODY

19. *Kinds of work, or functions of the plant.* — In accomplishing the purpose of its existence a plant is compelled to do a large number of different things, or carry on a variety of processes. Chief among these are the *absorption* of material from which food is to be formed from the soil and air; the *conversion* of these substances into compounds suitable for storage, transportation, or use by the protoplasm; the *assimilation* of the food into the living substance, *building up* and *enlarging* its body, *storing* up surplus food for future use, *conducting* water and other material from one part of its body to another, *digesting* the reserve material, such as starch, when needed for food, *breathing*, *throwing away* the worn-out and useless material, *holding* the body in the proper position, and finally, and most important of all, taking care that the species is preserved by giving rise to new individuals by means of *spores, seeds, runners,*

21

offsets, and other structures necessary for the process. In addition, the plant must use a large amount of energy and material in *protecting* all of its parts from injury or destruction by the climate, other plants, or by animals.

20. *Organs.* — In the lower or simpler plants, such as algæ and bacteria, all of these different things or functions are carried on by a very small body, often consisting of a single cell that could not be seen by the unaided eye. The whole body is used in carrying on nearly all of the various kinds of work. The "higher" plants are those which have developed separate portions of their bodies, especially suited to one or a few kinds of work. The part of a plant thus devoted to one or to a group of *functions* is termed an *organ*. Thus the *root, stem, leaf,* and *flower* are each responsible for certain kinds of work necessary for the welfare of the plant, and they are the principal organs of the higher plants.

21. *Tissues.* — If the structure of any of the organs is examined, it will be found that it is made up of a number of different kinds of material. Thus in an elder stem may be found *pith, wood, cambium,* and *bark.* The different masses are made up of dif-

ferent kinds of cells, and are called *tissues*. Every
tissue has a special share in the work of the organ
in which it occurs. The tendency of protoplasm to
divide its work among separate organs is one which
allows the living matter to carry on all of its
functions most economically and efficiently, and it
has been the chief principle in the development and
evolution of all living things.

22. *Method of study of functions and organs.*—
It will be found most convenient to take each organ
of the higher plants and learn what we may con-
cerning the work it does and the way in which it is
done. After a fair conception of the nature of the
activities of the plant has been gained in this manner, it will be possible to understand much more
clearly the mode of life of the simpler organisms in
which many kinds of work are carried on by the
same tissues or even by the same cell.

An insight of the special capacities of the separate
organs will also enable one to understand the work
in which the entire body of a higher plant par-
ticipates.

IV. THE ROOTS

23. *Functions of the roots.* — The higher plants are generally stationary, and do not move around except in the case of aquatics which float from place to place in currents of water. It was found in previous experiments that water which washed the soil in streams contains certain salts which it has extracted from the soil, and that these salts are necessary to make up the food of the plant. Furthermore, it will be seen by an examination of a few specimens that the roots are the organs which penetrate the soil to any depth, holding the plant in its place, and it is through these organs that food salts might be taken up. The root then may be credited with two kinds of work: *fixation* or *anchorage*, and *absorption of food.*

24. *Roots hold the stem firmly in position.* — Grasp the stem of a sunflower, or geranium, or some small plant, and attempt to pull it from the ground. A great amount of force will be necessary, as one

may easily learn in " weeding " a flower or garden bed. Try to uproot another specimen by pulling sidewise on the stem, and it will be found even more difficult to accomplish. Now tie a strong cord around the stem of a third specimen, and pass the cord over a thick branch of a tree or the top of a fence. Tie weights or heavy objects to the free end of the cord, and add to them until the plant is torn from the ground. How many pounds were necessary to do this ? If a strong pair of spring scales are at hand, this experiment may be performed more exactly. Tie the hook of the instrument to the upper part of the stem of a tomato or other small plant, and pull directly upward. Note the number of pounds indicated by the scale as the plant is torn loose. The plant is seen to come away with a mass of earth adhering to the roots. The roots are very plainly organs of fixation, and not only penetrate the soil, but clamp a large mass so that they may not be easily torn up. These organs anchor stems so securely that very heavy action of wind, water, or of animals is necessary to displace them. In a walk through a forest in which trees have been uprooted by storms, note the manner in which the masses of earth are clamped by the large roots and the general shape of the root system. What kinds of trees are most easily blown over?

25. *Roots were first developed for fixation.* — In the development of the plant world, roots were first formed by the protoplasm for the purpose of holding the organism in place, and in some of the simpler forms of plants there are to be seen species in which these organs serve no other purpose. The ribbonlike bodies of the marine seaweeds, the laminarias which may be a foot, or several hundred feet, in length, are fastened to the rocks by a system of " holdfasts," not much larger than the hand. The great extension of root systems to be seen in plants growing in the soil is chiefly for the purpose of absorption. If the root system of such a species is carefully dug up, it will be found to penetrate the soil to a depth of a few feet, and to extend out several feet from the base of the stem. Indeed, the total length of the root system generally exceeds that of the stems and branches. It has been found by actual measurement that the roots of a sunflower placed end to end would reach a distance of hundreds, and those of a squash thousands, of feet.

26. *Shrinkage of roots to aid in fixation.* — Examine the full-grown roots of a hyacinth (*Hyacinthus*), calla, or jack-in-the-pulpit (*Arisæma*). A short distance back of the tip the surface appears to be wrinkled. The wrinkling is due to the fact that the root elongates by growth at the tip, and as soon as any portion reaches a certain age, it shortens and causes little folds to appear on the surface tissue, or *epidermis*. If India-ink marks are placed on young roots, and the distance between them measured before and after wrinkling, it will be found that some shrink one-tenth or even one-fifth of their whole length. If the shrinkage of the root simply pulled it through the soil, it could be of no benefit to the plant and might work damage. The tip of the root, however, is firmly attached by means of the root-hairs, and then this portion is bent around so many small rocks that it is not easily pulled back by the contraction. As a result, the base or upper end of the root with the stem to which it is attached is pulled down into the soil still more firmly. Furthermore, if the root has sent out side branches, the soil between the side branches will be clamped between them in a manner well illustrated by the masses of rock and dirt seen adhering to the roots of pros-

trated trees. The side roots contract in the same manner so that the entire root system is a great complex clamp which grasps the soil and rocks very firmly, and thus greatly increases the anchoring power of the underground organs.

27. *The structure of the root.* — Examine an old root that has begun to decay. Material from a hyacinth or calla will be suitable. Hold the large end in one hand and strip off the outer delicate tissue, when a central cord or fibrous mass will be seen. When the organ is growing rapidly the outer cylinder of soft tissue absorbs water and expands, stretching the central fibrous cord as one might a rubber string. When the root grows old the outer tissues change their form, allowing the central cord to shorten, and wrinkling the epidermis in the process.

28. *Climbing roots.* — A large number of species of the higher plants form long slender stems which are unable to stand upright, and which are specially adapted for attachment to the trunks of trees and other tall objects, to which they are fastened by various methods. In many instances roots are developed many feet above the ground, and these adhere to the tree in various ways, holding the stem

securely in place. Here the original function of fixation alone is carried on, since generally no opportunity is offered to absorb food. So finely are these roots adapted for anchorage in difficult places that they can secure a foothold on the polished surface of a marble column or a sheet of glass. This may be seen in the ivy of the gardeners (*Ficus*).

29. *Stilt roots.* — A special adaptation of the fixative function is to be seen in the roots which start from the stem a short distance above the ground and extend outwardly and downwardly until they enter the soil several inches perhaps from the main stem. Such roots brace the stem, and if the tips form branches after entering the soil, their efficiency is still further increased. This may be seen in the wheat, corn, and other grasses, as well as in the palms and the mangroves. Go into a cornfield in early autumn and note the stilt roots. Pull a stalk sidewise and note their action.

30. *Columnar roots.* — In many of the forest trees, such as the beech, large roots are formed at the surface which take the form of an upright thick sheet of wood tapering in width toward the outer end where it is covered by the soil. These also

serve the purpose of bracing the stem against being blown over.

31. *Keel or ballast roots.* — Some aquatic plants are in the form of a leaflike stem or a *rosette* of leaves which floats on the surface of the water, and one or more roots are formed which hang downward in the water, serving to keep the floating parts in proper position, and perhaps also as organs of absorption. The members of the duckweed family (*Lemna*) and the water hyacinth are good examples of this, and should be examined.

32. *Substances of which the soil is composed.* — Examine a half cupful of soil taken from the garden, by means of a hand lens, or spread it out on a sheet of glass and hold in direct light. When separated into small portions with a needle it may be seen to be made up of irregular bodies of various sizes, bits of rock, fragments of leaves, stems, seed coats, splinters of bone, feathers, cast-off shards of beetles, as well as a variety of other matter which will depend on the locality from which the soil was taken. Every particle has a faint shiny appearance which disappears more or less completely if the mass is dried over a hot stove. The shiny appearance was

due to a thin layer of water which surrounded each particle. It is this thin layer of water which is taken up by the plant, and it contains the mineral salts of the soil in solution.

33. *The soil and root-hairs adhere.* — If the specimens which were torn up were examined, it would have been seen, that in addition to the masses of soil clamped by the roots, there was a thin layer immediately surrounding each separate root which did not come away easily. Pull up a young bean plant or any other that may be convenient, and examine the roots with a hand lens. The minute particles of soil are seen to be adherent to small glistening hairs which arise from the root, rather than to the surface of the root itself.

34. *Root-hairs and the region from which they arise.* — The root-hairs are very delicate in structure, and it may be seen very readily that they are not found along the entire extent of the root. A better view of these organs may be seen if some are grown where they may not adhere to any solid particles which partially hide them. To do this, cut a circular piece of blotting-paper the size of the bottom of a plate, soak it in water, and lay it in a plate. Drop

a dozen seeds of wheat or oats or radish on the blotting-paper and cover with a glass dish. After germination has proceeded for two or three days, take
up one of the seedlings and hold between the window and the eye. Innumerable fine hairs are seen
projecting from the roots on all sides. If these
were examined with a hand lens, they would be seen
to be small tubes. Compare the number of root-
hairs near the tip with those of the basal portion of
the root : where are they most plentiful ? The tubes
are the shape of a finger of a glove, and when thrust
in among the hard particles of the soil they take
irregular shapes and adhere very closely to the bodies
they touch, as may be seen if a thin layer of sand
is placed on · the paper at the beginning of the
experiment.

35. *Action of roots which have been deprived of
hairs.* — Perhaps the best method of illustration of
the uses of root-hairs is to note the action of a
root from which they have been taken. To do this
remove a young sunflower plant from the ground
and shake and brush all of the soil from the roots.
This will carry off all the root-hairs, but if performed carefully, will not otherwise injure the roots.

Replace the plant in the soil as it was before. It will be seen to wilt, no matter how much water is poured over it. From this it is fair to conclude that a root from which the hairs have been broken cannot absorb enough water to meet the needs of all the leaves and stems.

The root-hairs serve the general purpose of increasing the amount of absorbing surface of the root, and as a general rule they are most plentiful on the roots of species growing in dry soils, and are almost wholly absent from species growing in wet soils, swamps, or in the water.

36. *Can water be taken in through the leaves?* — Plants which are slightly wilted often revive when the leaves are sprinkled. The wetting of the leaves might be of benefit to the plant in two ways: it might prevent them from drying out by losing the small supply of water they are receiving from the roots, or it might allow them to absorb water like the roots. It is popularly supposed that leaves may take up water, and the following test will throw some light on the matter. Place a young potted specimen of geranium or tomato where it may not receive water until it has wilted from thirst. In-

D

vert the pot, and sprinkle the leaves with water four or five times in an hour Does it recover from wilting? Place the plant upright and water soil copiously: note result. Repeat the test with other plants and determine the matter fully. Can a plant absorb water from the air in sufficient quantity for its needs through its leaves?

Still another method for testing the capacity of the leaf for absorbing water consists in floating a wilted leaf of the fuchsia or begonia in a vessel of water, with the upper surface downward, and noting results.

37. *The manner in which root-hairs take up liquids.* — If you were to place some water on one side of a piece of wet parchment, and some sugar on the opposite side, it would be seen that the water would go through the parchment to the sugar in a very short time. It is by a similar action that root-hairs take water from the soil. The root-hair has the form of the finger of a glove with the walls made of parchment. It is lined with living matter, and is filled with water containing sugar and acids. When the hair touches the thin film of water surrounding the particles of soil

the soil water is drawn through the walls into the cavity in the same manner as through the parchment. Besides this attractive power of the solution inside the root-hair, the thin layer of living matter lining the wall is of such nature that it attracts water, and it will allow the passage of soil water containing mineral substances; but will not permit the escape of any of the liquid containing sugar, except in the most minute quantities. The small amount of acid which does escape is seen to act very strongly on the rocks in the soil (§ 40).

38. *Action of sugar.* — The manner in which sugar draws water into the root-hair is illustrated by the following method: Cut away the top of a carrot, and dig out a cavity as large as an acorn. Fill the cavity with dry sugar and set aside for a few hours The sugar will be converted into sirup, having drawn water through the walls of the cells of the carrot.

39. *Another method of imitation of the action of root-hairs.* — Select a long, sound potato, and bore a cavity in it reaching from one end nearly to the other, being careful not to split it. Trim the skin from the closed end and shape it so that it will stand

upright in a saucer of water an inch deep. Fill
the cavity with sugar. Examine five or six hours
later. The sugar will have drawn the soil water
from the saucer through the wall and filled up the
cavity perhaps to overflowing in a very close imitation of the action of a root-hair.

40. *Action of root-hairs on particles of mineral
substance.* — The root-hairs take up the thin film of
water surrounding each particle of soil, and as the
walls of the hair are constantly saturated with acid
or other substances which will corrode rock, they
also dissolve some of it in such manner that it can
be absorbed. To demonstrate this action fill a small
flower-pot half full of common garden loam, and on
top of it lay a piece of marble, an oyster or clam
shell with a polished surface uppermost. Cover with
three inches of clean sand. Place one or two beans
in the sand, and water from day to day. After a
few days the seeds germinate and send down roots
through the soil, which come in contact with the
marble or the shells. Two weeks later remove the
marble or shell, wash clean, wipe, and allow to dry.
Hold between the eye and a window in such manner
that the surface will be seen by a reflected light.

Irregular branching lines or roughened areas will show where the roots have touched the polished surface, and the hairs have *etched* away the mineral.

41. *The fate of the particles of the soil.* — The particles of soil may be roughly classed as *mineral* and *organic*. The latter comprise the remains of plants and animals as described above, and constitute what is known as *humus*. The humus is constantly being broken down by the action of the soil bacteria and other minute organisms. This action of the bacteria is to obtain the material necessary for their own food, and in the process great quantities of substance are formed which the higher plants use. The deep layer of decaying leaves and twigs in a forest that has not been burned, or laid bare by grazing animals, is a good example of humus formation.

The mineral particles may not be said to decay, but they are constantly being broken up. The water in the soil always contains *carbonic acid* set free by living plants and by the action of bacteria on the humus, as well as by the decomposition of certain minerals themselves. Other acids are found in the air and are washed down into the soil by rains. The thin film of water which surrounds each particle con-

tains these acids, and slowly eats away the outer
layers, and wherever the roots or their hairs touch,
the corrosion is increased so that each small particle
in time is entirely dissolved. The rock particles
would thus soon disappear from the soil, but fragments are constantly being split from the larger
rocks by the action of frost, and heat, and the rend-
ing action of large roots, so that the supply is kept up.

42. *Food material in the soil and how the plant
finds it.* — The substances which are formed by the
corrosion of the rocks and the decay of humus are
not found everywhere in the same quantity, but are
scattered more or less unevenly through the soil.
To be of the greatest service to the plant, therefore,
the roots must not only absorb substances, but
should be able to find the places where they are
most abundant. The roots of the higher plants are
capable of doing this, and direct their tips into the
places which contain the food and water necessary
for the plant. In order to be able to accomplish this,
these organs have become sensitive to gravity, light,
heat, moisture, and chemical substances. Some of
the forms of sensitiveness of the root may be easily
observed.

43. *The tips of primary or main roots point downward.* — Germinate some peas or beans, as in § 34, and when the first roots are two or three inches in length, thrust a pin through the seeds and fasten to a piece of wood or cork with the tips pointing directly upward. Float the cork or wood in a saucer of water and cover with an inverted tumbler. Examine two to four hours later. The tip will generally be found to be pointing downward, having curved near the apex. This behavior is due to its *sensitiveness* to gravity. The root tends to place its axis in a position in which the tip is directed toward the centre of the earth. This movement is not caused by the weight of the root, and it does not bend like a piece of soft wax, as may be seen if you attempt to bend it back to its original position. It breaks in consequence of such forcible bending. The curvature of the root is due to the action of certain definite parts designed to do such work.

44. *The tips of branches of the main roots are directed horizontally.* — The downward growth and extension of the first roots formed by a seedling is a necessity for almost all plants After the main root has bored down into the soil, it finds the food

substances distributed equally in all directions from
it. To secure this the branches drive their tips
horizontally or nearly so, taking a course nearly
parallel to the surface of the soil. The positions
attained by these secondary roots may be seen if a
young bean or tomato plant is carefully dug from
the ground, noting the position of the main roots
and the branches as they are exposed to view.

45. *Sensitiveness of the roots to moisture.* — Both
lateral and main roots may encounter other forces,
which cause them to bend away from the directions taken in response to gravity as described in
the previous paragraphs. The action of unevenly
distributed moisture may be shown as follows: Place
some germinating peas in a deep cigar box full of
garden soil. They should be planted in the ordinary manner near the middle of the box. Give the
seedlings barely enough water to keep the soil moist
at one end of the box. Pour the necessary amount
from a cup on the soil just inside one end and allow
it to diffuse toward the plants. The quantity should
be so small that the soil in the other end of the box
will become quite dry. After a growth of two weeks
turn the box upside down, shake out the plant, and

observe the position of the roots. Note the direction of the tips, and compare the number and length of those in the moist end of the box with those in the other end. This sensitiveness of roots to moisture, by which they are attracted toward it, causes cisterns and drains to become filled with the roots of clovers, grasses, willows, and elms.

46. *Roots bend away from light.* — The course taken by roots in response to gravity and moisture usually leads them deeper into the soil and away from the light, but they have the power of bending away toward darkness if the soil should be taken from above them. This may be demonstrated in the following manner: Tie a piece of muslin over a tumbler and punch a number of holes in it with a bodkin. Fill the tumbler completely full with water. Lay some germinating seeds of the radish on the muslin with the roots directed through the holes in the cloth. Set in a window where it may receive a strong light. Add enough water daily to keep the vessel full. Observe the positions of the roots from day to day. The tips will be seen to be directed away from the point from which the light comes, and they crowd toward the inner side of the tumbler.

47. *The tip of the root is protected by a sheath-ing cap.* — The delicate tip of the root is pushed through the soil very rapidly, and its apex must be protected or it would be torn by the rough edges of the rock particles. This may be readily realized when it is found that the pressure by which the root is driven forward is equal to fifteen or twenty atmospheres, or two or three hundred pounds to the square inch, much greater than that exerted by steam in a locomotive boiler.

If the root meets a soft or yielding substance, it bores through it precisely as you might push a large needle through the same mass. The young roots of rapidly growing plants are often seen to penetrate soft or decaying wood, or even the large roots of other plants. The actual tip of the root proper is composed of extremely delicate cells, with the thinnest coverings in the way of cell walls, and they would be crushed by the lightest touch of any hard object. These cells are of importance because by their division the tissues of the new portions of the root are formed. To protect the delicate mass of living matter most roots are furnished with a *sheath* or *cap* on the tip. This root-cap has come to serve other purposes as well, and it may be

found on aquatics covering the tips of roots which
hang down in the water and do not touch any hard
object.   In such examples the sheath is generally
very long, extending back over the younger portion
of the root, and as it is filled with bitter substances
it prevents swimming animals from eating or injuring the tips of the roots.   It may be seen with
difficulty on land plants, but on aquatics, such as
the water hyacinth, it is a fourth of an inch long,
and may be pulled off and examined with the eye,
or better by the aid of a hand lens.   A sketch of
the appearance of the root should be made, and a
number of species should be examined in search
for this protecting cap.

48. *The sensitiveness of roots to touch or contact
with solid objects.* — The root-cap would not be sufficient to protect the tip of the root from all danger
of injury if it were pushed forward in a straight
line and did not turn aside for an obstruction   As
a means of avoiding injury from this cause the
root has become sensitive to the touch or contact
of hard objects, in such manner that it bends away
from them.   This may be seen by the repetition
of one of Darwin's classical experiments.   Fix a

seedling to a cork, as in § 43, using a very long pin, but placing the root with the tip pointing downward but not touching the water or the cork. Now cut the smallest bit of paper you can handle, and fasten to one side of the extreme tip by means of gum arabic softened in water, or shellac. Observe four or five hours, and a day later, and the apex of the root will be seen to have curved away from the side to which the paper was attached, exactly as it would bend away from a hard object in its path. Some difficulty may be experienced in attaching the paper properly, and the experiment should be repeated until some decisive result is at hand.

49. *The roots of air plants.* — There are a large number of species which inhabit the warmer countries that never reach the soil, but live upon the branches of trees, to which they cling by means of climbing roots, such as were mentioned in § 28. They also form long cordlike roots which hang downward sometimes twenty or even forty feet in length, with the diameter of a lead pencil. In some instances these reach the soil, and then branches are formed. Generally, however, these *aërial* roots are papery white in color and have a

curious crinkled appearance, especially in the case of orchids. This is due to the peculiar structure of the outer layers of cells. In fact, these roots have a layer of tissue not found in ordinary roots. This outer tissue is composed of cells, which die as soon as they attain full size, and the walls are left, forming a layer of loose spongy tissue entirely sheathing the root. The *spongy* layer not only absorbs drops of water which may fall upon it, but will also gather water from the air when it is humid and damp. The species furnished with such roots usually live in localities which have much rain, and their entire supply of water may be gathered in these ways.

50. *Parasitic roots.* — Many species have the habit of fastening to the bodies of other plants and drawing a part or all of their water and food from them. They do not need the ordinary soil roots, but have developed special forms which are capable of piercing the bodies of their hosts, as the plants on which they live are called. The mistletoe is an example of this type; but perhaps the *parasite* most widely distributed in America is the dodder (*Cuscuta*), which may be seen in damp

meadows in July and August, twining around the stems of almost any herbaceous plant, forming numerous coils of yellow or cream-colored flowers. If the host plant is taken up and the nature of the union between the two is examined, it will be seen that the parasitic dodder sends a large number of small blunt projections or knobs of tissue into the stem of the host.   These are the roots, and they may arise at any point on the stem of the dodder, and their function is the absorption of the sap of the host plant.

51. *Method of germination and growth of the dodder.* — The seed of the dodder germinates on the ground, sending up a long threadlike stem which waves about slowly in the air until its tip comes in contact with the stem of another species, when it coils around it and sends out its roots.   The roots are seen to arise only at points where the parasite touches the stem of the host.   If the seed of the dodder is planted in a pot with a young tomato plant or castor oil plant, this may be observed.   It may be seen also that the only root formed at the base of the stem on the germination of the seed is a short peg-shaped structure, and that it simply holds

the seedling in place until it has found a host to which it can fasten. As soon as this is accomplished, the soil root and the lower part of the stem of the dodder dies away, leaving it entirely supported on the body of its host.

52. *Union of roots with fungi.* — Quite a large number of the higher plants form what are known as *mycorrhizas*. A mycorrhiza is the structure which results from the union of roots or absorbing organs with the tubelike hyphæ or threads of a mushroom or mould in the soil. This union is of benefit to both the fungus and the higher plant. In some instances the fungus lives inside the root, and in others it forms a layer of threads on the outside.

If the smaller roots of the beech, oak, or any of the pines are dug up, a number of short club-shaped branches may be seen which are brownish in color These short branches are inhabited by fungi and are mycorrhizas. A second example may be sought for in the waxy white " Indian pipe " or " corpse plant " (*Monotropa*) which grows in deep woods. Its short bunches of curiously shaped roots are covered with a layer of felt made up of the threads of the fungus. The higher plant gets practically all of its food from the fungus, and it therefore has no need of true green leaves. It has lost these organs in times past because of the very fact that it ceased to use them. It is true of all living things, that as soon as an organ ceases to be used or to be useful, it is developed less perfectly on each succeeding generation of individuals until perhaps only a rudiment remains. This is illustrated by the coral-root (*Corallorhiza*), a reddish orchid common throughout the Northern states. This plant has not only reduced its leaves, but on account of the activity of the fungus in supplying it with food, the roots have been entirely lost, the fungus of the mycorrhizas now living in the short underground stems which have the appearance of a bunch of coral.

53. *Roots as storage organs.* — During the summer season the plant manufactures much more food than it can use at that time, and the surplus is stored up until needed. The amount thus accumulated is often sufficient to feed the plant through several successive seasons in case it had no opportunity to make its usual supply. Various parts of the body are selected as places of storage. The beet is an example of a root and a small portion of a stem be-

ing used for the storage of sugar. The sweet potato family deposit the reserve food in the form of starch in the roots, which become extremely large, as may be seen in the cultivated form. One of this family, the " man of the earth " (*Ipomea pandurata*), enlarges the main root and deposits starch and oil in it until it reaches a length of several feet, a diameter of six to eight inches, and weighs as much as twenty pounds. It is to be borne in mind that not all parts of the plant found underground are roots. Many species have stems which live very much like roots and resemble them in general appearance. They may be separated from them, however, by the absence of the root-cap, and by the fact that they show *joints,* or *nodes,* and produce *buds,* although the roots of the sweet potato are also capable of giving rise to buds.

54. *Method of growth of roots.* — Another feature which distinguishes roots from stems is the method of growth. Germinate a pea or bean, as shown in § 34, until the main root is two or three inches long, then mark it off in sections a quarter of an inch long by means of lines of India-ink applied by means of a thread or a thin splinter of wood.

E

Measure the distance between the marks daily for a week. In what part of the root does most of the growth take place? Compare with the growth of roots (§ 54), leaves (§ 113), and stems (§§ 144–151).

55. *Absorbing and fixing organs of the lower plants.* — Roots represent the most highly perfected organs for the fixation of the plant in its position and the absorption of food. In the lower forms, incapable of building such complex organs, these functions must be carried on by simpler structures, which perhaps must take other and additional work.

56. *Absorbing and fixing organs of the ferns, mosses, and liverworts.* — Among the ferns, mosses, and liverworts absorption and fixation are carried on chiefly by means of large tubes termed *rhizoids*, which resemble root-hairs except in size and heaviness of the walls, although rootlike organs are present in some species. Some of these forms are very much like the higher plants, in which instance the large rhizoids are attached to the underground parts like root-hairs. In other instances the plant is in the form of a leaflike body, which lies on the surface of the ground. The rhizoids spring directly from

the lower side of the flattened body and penetrate the soil, accomplishing both fixation and absorption Each little tube is very delicate, yet their combined strength is sufficient to hold the body quite firmly in position. The thin bodies of the ordinary liverwort (*Marchantia polymorpha* or *Conocephalus*) should be examined and the character of the rhizoids noted. They will be seen as a tangled mass, to which are adhering great numbers of particles of soil.

57. *Method of fixation of the moulds and mushrooms.* — Find a number of freshly grown mushrooms or "toadstools" in the ground in the woods, and carefully dig away the soil from around the base of. the stalk supporting the umbrella-like top. Running away from the base of this stalk are a number of ragged-looking grayish strands, and if these are followed out farther, they will be seen to divide and subdivide into still smaller strands. These strands constitute the absorbing and fixing part of the plant, and they are made up of a great number of tubes. Bundles of tubes branch off separately and in small groups all along the main strands, giving them the peculiar ragged appearance. These organs penetrate the soil to great distances, living and growing during

all of the warm season, absorbing the substances set free by the decay of other plants. At certain times they send up the large branches which are ordinarily know as mushrooms, which bear innumerable *spores,* and which reproduce the plant. The *mycelium,* or mass of tubes, spreads rapidly underground, and the mushrooms may appear in the most unexpected places and very suddenly. Like the roots of the higher plants, they are driven upward through the soil with great force, and may be seen to lift stones, large pieces of wood, or heavy clods of earth. Mushrooms have been known to grow up under the stones of the sidewalks in village streets, lifting them from their places and seriously disarranging the pavement.

58. *Absorption and fixation by the algæ, and bacteria.* — Many of the plants of the lowest groups are completely submerged in water in which their food is dissolved, and as a consequence they absorb food over their entire surfaces. Some of these, especially the bacteria, are in the form of small globular or egg-shaped cells, or in the form of rods joined together in a chain, all floating freely in the water. The function of fixation is clearly absent in most

instances, and absorption is carried on by the entire body. Some of these organisms accomplish fixation in certain stages of their existence by means of jelly-like substances outside their walls. Some of these floating forms run out minute threads of protoplasm, with which they lash the water in such manner as to swim from place to place. Others, with single or many celled bodies, make *holdfasts*, or fixing roots, with which they attach themselves to the rocks or the bottom of the pond or stream.

A general idea of the nature of these organisms may be gained by an examination of the pond-scums (*Spirogyra*), which float near the surface, and are made up of a number of long threads, each thread being formed by the division and growth of numbers of rod-shaped green cells.

V. THE LEAVES

59. *Structure of leaves.*—Examine the leaves of the oak, maple, beech, and willow on the stems. The leaf will be found to consist of three principal parts: the *base* or portion by which it is attached to the stem, the stalk or *petiole,* and the blade or *lamina.* The base may take the form of a swelling of the petiole, as in the locust, bean, or sumach, or it may develop small, leaflike appendages, as in the willow. Make an examination of the leaf of the willow and draw to show results of observations.

The petiole is generally in the form of a stalk or stem, though it may be edged or winged, or it may be absent, in which case the lamina of the leaf sits directly on the stem. Find some plant the leaves of which are lacking in petioles, and draw.

The base and the petiole are for the purpose of supporting the lamina in the proper position, and conducting water and food to it. It is in the lamina that the most important work of the leaf is done,

Now make a careful examination of the blades of the leaves you have brought together. Trace the exact outlines on a piece of paper. Are the margins cut to the same pattern? Compare the upper and lower sides of the leaves. The upper side is fairly smooth and even, while the lower is rougher and shows numbers of ridges or *nerves*, which may be seen only faintly on the upper side. Fill out the outline of each leaf with a tracing of the nerves. It will be found that the nerves start from the base of the leaf or from a median *midrib* and divide and subdivide, running to all parts of the blade. The space between the nerves is filled by a soft green tissue, the *mesophyl*, and the nerves serve as a framework to hold it in position. By searching among the beds of dead leaves in the woods old specimens may be found from which the mesophyl has decayed, leaving the network of the nerves almost entire. The lower surface of the leaf is furnished with thousands of minute openings, the *stomata*. These are usually so small that they may not be seen even with a hand lens; but if some of the flattish fronds of the liverwort (*Conocephalus*) can be found, they may be seen on the upper surface with the naked eye.

The entire leaf, as well as that of the body of the seed-plant, is covered with a thin sheet of cells, the *epidermis*. The epidermis may be peeled off in whitish strips by using a needle, or point of a sharp knife.

60. *Leaves with both surfaces alike.* — The leaves examined in the preceding paragraph are held in a horizontal position on the stems. Examine leaves that are held in an upright position or nearly so, like those of the narcissus, iris, or lily. The nerves will not be so apparent, and both surfaces present nearly the same appearance and would show about the same arrangement of the cells.

61. *Compound leaves.* — Examine the leaves of the locust, pea, bean, or sumach. The three principal parts may be found, but the lamina appears to be branched or cut up into a number of smaller *leaflets*, each with its own stalk by which it is fastened to the midrib or *rhachis* of the leaf. The number of leaflets in the bean is three (see also § 217). Determine the number in the locust, pea, and other specimens you may find. The compound leaf is capable of doing more work than the simple forms showing the same extent of lamina.

62. *Composition of the air.* — The leaves are generally held aloft in the air, and since they come into contact with no other medium, it is plain that the composition of the air will be of great interest to any one studying the activity of leaves. The air is made up of nitrogen, carbonic acid gas, oxygen, argon, and perhaps other rare gases in small quantities. Besides, watery vapor, and traces of acids are present in a proportion which varies greatly with the locality. In 10,000 gallons of ordinary air would be found about 7795 gallons of nitrogen, 2061 gallons of oxygen, 4 gallons of carbon dioxide, 140 gallons of water, and small amounts of the other constituents. These gases and vapors are not united to form a compound. Thus hydrogen and oxygen are united to form the compound water, but the gases of the air are simply mixed together without actually uniting.

63. *Gases of use to the plant.* — The oxygen and carbon dioxide are of the greatest importance to the plant. Nitrogen of the air is of no use, except to mix with and dilute the other gases. Only a few species are capable of taking this gas and using it as food. This element is usually gained from compounds in the soil.

The water of the air is rarely used by the plant, yet its presence prevents the plant from drying out, and it is of great importance in this way. The other substances are more or less useful or harmful, according to the quantities present.

64. *Functions of the leaf.* — To the leaf is intrusted the work of taking in the carbon dioxide of the air, splitting it up, and combining it with water sent up from the roots, in such manner as to form sugars. The stream of water also brings up mineral substances from the roots which are needed in the leaf. The amount of water which thus reaches the leaf is much greater than can be used in the tissues, and most of it must be thrown off. This is also done by the leaf.

65. *The colors of leaves.* — The leaves of most species are colored green by the presence of a substance the botanist terms *chlorophyl*, and this pigment is also found in the outer tissues of some stems, branches, or even roots. It is formed in special masses of protoplasm, and the depth of the green color of the leaf depends on the number of these masses in the cells. Then again the living matter

has the power of moving the masses of pigment toward and away from the surface so that the tone of color may change in the same leaf during the course of a few hours.

Besides the green, other coloring matter may be present in the cells, or the walls may be dyed. The leaf may show a certain color because of the contents of its cells, or because of the color of its walls, in the same manner that a bottle of liquid may appear blue because of the color of the liquid, or the tint of the glass

66. *Hidden chlorophyl.* — Chlorophyl may be hidden because of the presence of other colors. The leaves of the amaranth, cockscomb, and many other species appear to be dark red in color, and no chlorophyl is to be seen. That it is present, however, may be shown by the following experiment. Place a colored leaf as above, in a dish of cold water, and bring it to a boil over a stove or spirit lamp. If this is continued for a few minutes, the red color will be extracted, and the normal green of the leaf will be visible. The experiment also shows that red coloring matter is soluble in water, while chlorophyl is not.

67. *Characteristics of chlorophyl.*—Chlorophyl is absolutely indispensable for the formation of food in the leaf, and it will be important to extract some of it from a leaf and ascertain its qualities. To do this place a number of leaves, that have been cut up into small pieces or bruised, in a bottle or tumbler and cover with alcohol. Close the vessel and set away in a dark place for a day. Pour off some of the liquid into a wine-glass or small test tube. Hold up to the light. The solution appears to be of a bright emerald green. Now hold the glass in direct sunlight and look at the edge of the liquid. If held properly, it will show a blazing red appearance. Chlorophyl has the power of making such changes in sunlight that it appears red; it affects light in other ways also.

68. *Spectrum of chlorophyl.*—If the study of chlorophyl were continued in the physical laboratory, it could be seen that if light which has passed through a solution of chlorophyl is spread out on a screen by means of a prism of glass, some of the colors of the artificial rainbow will be missing. The missing parts will comprise the blue, violet, and most of the red rays. Chlorophyl, in the living plant, ab-

sorbs these rays, and the energy derived from them enables protoplasm to carry on the work of food-making.

69. *The leaf is a machine or a mill.* — If the activity of chlorophyl might be described in another way, it could be said that the leaf is an engine. The chlorophyl would be the boiler, and when light falls upon it energy or power is set free, which causes the engine to move or perform work, as when heat is applied to the boiler of a steam engine. The leaf is a solar engine and gets its energy from light instead of heat rays. The power acquired from light by chlorophyl drives the protoplasmic machinery and enables it to take water and carbon dioxide and make sugar from them, throwing off certain things not used in the process. After the formation of sugar it is combined with nitrogen and other elements before it can become a part of the living matter.

70. *Quality of light most useful to the plant.* — Prepare two boxes of seedlings. The boxes should be at least six or eight inches deep, and the plants should be grown in a thin layer of soil at the bottom of the box. Cover one box with a sheet of win-

dow glass and red tissue paper, and the other with glass and blue paper, and set in a sunny place. Care for the plants from day to day, and compare their growth at the end of a week. This will determine whether the blue or red rays are most useful to the plant, and will also recall the mistaken "blue glass" craze of a few years ago.

71. *Light destroys chlorophyl.* — Place a portion of the solution of chlorophyl prepared in § 67 in the sunlight, and the remainder in a dark closet. Compare the color of the two in a few days. The one in the light will be seen to have faded. The fading action of light goes on in the leaf constantly, but the green color is constantly restored by the protoplasm. If a plant should be exposed to a light much stronger than that to which it is accustomed, the fading will take place faster than the living matter could mend it, and the leaf would turn yellow and die.

72. *Light is necessary for the formation of chlorophyl in most instances.* — While light slowly breaks down chlorophyl, yet the plant usually cannot form its substance without the aid of light. Place a bulb of canna, jack-in-the-pulpit, or a seed of the

pea or bean in proper soil in a pot and set in a dark cellar and then cover with a bucket or a box. Give the seedling the proper amount of water, which will be less than if grown in light. After a time shoots will be formed which will be very much different from those grown from similar seedlings or plants in the light.

Lay a broad board on the grass, and note the color of the blades beneath a week later. Not only will the chlorophyl be absent, but the stems and leaves will be greatly changed in form and size. The stems will be two or three times as long as usual. This seems to be a method by which the plant gets its leaves and stems up to sunlight when they are covered by anything or overshadowed by other plants. Species like the narcissus, which have sword-shaped leaves with no petiole or stem above ground, elongate the blade of the leaf itself in this effort to get up to light.

73. *Capacity of leaves for the absorption of light.* —Take any tube of wood, metal, or paper an inch or more in diameter, and fasten a leaf over the end. This may be done by turning the margins back over the tube and tying a string around the tube at that

point. Hold the tube with this end pointing directly toward the sun, and put the eye at the other end. Can any light be seen through the leaf? If so, add another leaf and test again. How many leaves are necessary to take up all the light? If several kinds of leaves are tested in this way, it will be found that those of different species vary greatly in their light-absorbing power. Do you notice any connection between this capacity and the place in which the species grows naturally?

74. *Formation of food in chlorophyl-bearing organs.* — The carbon dioxide of the air is used by the plant in making food. This compound consists of two volumes of oxygen and one of carbon. It is taken into the leaf through openings on the lower surface and passes through the thin walls of the cells containing chlorophyl. It is then split in two parts, and the carbon is combined with the oxygen and hydrogen of water to form a sugar. Most of the oxygen is thrown off. All of these steps may not be followed, even in the best-equipped laboratory, but if the leaf of any water plant growing in the sunlight is observed, it may be seen to give off small bubbles of oxygen. This may be best seen by plac-

ing a small aquatic plant in a tumbler, or the leaf of a land plant may be immersed in water and the formation of the bubbles noted.

75. *Non-green colors.* — If the experiment in § 72 is repeated, it may be seen that red and other colors are formed in leaves grown in darkness as well as in light. This may be illustrated still further if a flowering branch of some plant is thrust through a hole in the wall of a tight pasteboard box, and the flowers allowed to open in darkness. The most noticeable of the colors that are found in leaves, beside green, is red, though purples are also abundant. All shades of red, blue, and yellow are to be seen in flowers and fruits. If a clump of rhubarb is made to grow in a dark cellar, the leaves and stems will be blood red.

76. *Origin of red colors.* — Red coloring matter is formed most freely in parts of the plant containing much sugar. The origin of coloring matters is not well understood. It has been determined, however, that when a specimen is fed with sugar, it will manufacture this color more abundantly. To demonstrate this action a species should be selected that has the power of making the color, such as ivy,

F

Virginia creeper, columbine; and a cutting composed of a large branch or twig should have the lower end immersed in a stone or glass jar as in the water cultures previously described, § 13.   The jars should be filled with water from a stream or well to which an ounce of sugar or glucose has been added for each quart.   Compare the colors of the leaves with others grown in the same kind of water without sugar, and also with those remaining on the plant.

This experiment may be repeated if living specimens of the bladderwort (*Utricularia*) can be procured.   Place some specimens in a shallow dish of water and set in the sun.   Prepare a second dish, but add the proportion of sugar used in the last test. Change the liquids at least once a week.   Note the depth of red color of the two specimens.   Cold and wounds also induce the formation of red coloring matter.

77. *Changes in color.* — The red and blue colors appear to be very closely connected, because the parts of a plant may often change from one to the other in the course of a few days.   This may be noticed in the flowers of the peony, as well as in the opening buds of many plants.   Note the color of

the leaves of the oak and maple immediately after the buds open in the spring, and compare with that of the mature organs. Compare also the colors of ripe and unripe fruits, such as apples, tomatoes, berries, plums, and peaches.

78. *Autumnal colors.* — The colors of autumnal leaves are very striking, not only because of their depth and brilliancy, but because they appear on so many leaves and so many plants at the same time. Furthermore, the plants which show colors most notably are trees which are large and prominent features of the landscape. These colors embrace a large number of shades and tints of yellow, red, and purple, and they are probably formed from the sugar in the cells, and by the breaking down of the green color into yellows and browns. Yellow colors are also formed independently, or appear most strikingly in dying leaves. The actual changes of color in at least one species should be followed through the months of September and October, as well as the colors of the same species when the buds open in the following spring. Although the autumnal colors of every species show some diversity, yet the keynote is fairly constant. The birches are a golden yellow,

the oaks vary through yellow orange to reddish brown, the red maple is generally a scarlet varying to a dark red, the tulip tree a light yellow, and sumachs become a flaming scarlet. These colors show some variation with the amount of moisture and character of the soil.

79. *Uses of autumnal colors.* — The actual purpose of the autumnal colors cannot be determined. There is no doubt, however, that their presence prevents damage by sunlight to delicate substances which are withdrawn from the leaf to the stem before they are cast off.

80. *Uses of red and other colors in flowers and fruits.* — The purpose of the brilliant colors of flowers, fruits, and leaves is not clearly made out. The colors of flowers may serve to attract insects, but this is the case in only a few instances An insect is attracted to a flower generally by the scent of nectar or honey, and it recognizes the flower by its size and form rather than by the color. The same is true of fruits which need the aid of insects for their dissemination. It is to be noted that very vivid colors are often found in the centre of large

objects, such as the sugar beet, or large fruits, where they could not possibly be of any use whatever.

81. *Characteristics of red and blue colors.* — It has been shown in § 66 that the red color of a leaf of coleus may be extracted by water, and it is a matter of common experience that the colors of fruits are easily obtained in this way. If red coloring matter is examined in the same manner as chlorophyl, it will be found that it absorbs different rays of light than those taken up by the green pigment.

82. *Red color as a shield.* — A great many species are furnished with a layer of red color on the upper side of the leaf. This absorbs some of the light which strikes the leaf, and a diminished amount is allowed to fall upon the delicate green coloring matter below. The action of the red then would be like the slats of a shutter, which permit only a part of the rays to shine through. The presence of the red would be beneficial to leaves exposed to a degree of sunlight stronger than they are otherwise adapted to bear.

83. *Red color as a heat producer.* — The rays of light that are taken up by the red and blue colors are converted into heat. This may be demonstrated if two naked-bulb thermometers are procured. Next find a species which has some of its leaves green and others red, such as canna or coleus. Wrap a green leaf around the bulb of one and secure it with a small string. Place a red leaf around the bulb of the second instrument. Expose them side by side to the sunlight for twenty minutes, then read the height of the mercury in both instruments.

84. *Red color as a heat saver.* — Examine a number of plants growing in a deep forest in the shade. Many of those species which have large leaves lying against the ground, or floating on the water, will exhibit a layer of color on the lower side of the leaf but none on the upper. Light which strikes such leaves will be used partly by the chlorophyl, and the remainder on reaching the lower side of the leaf will be mostly converted into heat by the red pigment. Again, it is to be said that it is not definitely known that the color is formed here for that purpose. The color may be produced as a result of the fact that it is subjected to low temperatures at night, but it certainly does bear the above relation to light.

85. *Hairs as a protection to the leaf.* — The leaves of many species, especially those growing in localities subject to very intense sunlight, are often clothed with a dense layer of long wavy or branching hairs, and these serve to ward off the fiercer rays and prevent drying out. The same purpose is also accomplished by the development of a very heavy outer *cuticle* or wall of the epidermis.

86. *White flowers.* — The white colors of flowers or other portions of the plant are due to entirely different causes Chief among these is the loose arrangement of the cells and the absence of coloring matter. The air between the cells reflects back the light, giving the whitish effect This may be illustrated by the appearance of a sheet of glass when unbroken, and when crushed or pounded into minute particles. In the first case it shows its natural color and is transparent. When pounded up into a mass of sand-like particles, the light is reflected back from the surface of each, giving the mass a whitish appearance. Test the paper-white leaves of any plant you may be able to obtain from a greenhouse and determine to what extent the light penetrates them, as in § 73.

87. *The positions of leaves.* — Go out into an open woods or meadow and note the positions of the leaves of all the plants you may see. Select a suitable specimen and walk around it, noting the positions of these organs on every side of the plant. Do they face all the points of the compass? are they horizontal? Do you note any connection between their position and that from which the rays of light come? Does every leaf receive direct sunlight at some time of the day, and at the same hour?

88. *Length of the petioles.* — Take a number of leaves from different parts of the same plant, and compare the length of the petioles. Observe the leaves as they are attached to the stems. Does this inequality of the petiole serve any purpose in connection with the light? Take the long-petioled leaves from some plant and put them in the place of short-petioled leaves on another stem. What is the result, so far as receiving light is concerned?

89. *Leaf mosaic.* — A close examination will show that length of stalk and size of blade stand in close relation to each other, and that the distance between the points at which the leaves are fastened to the stems is also a factor in their arrangement.

The full effect of each factor may be seen if the arrangement of the leaves of the ivy or some plant which clings closely to a wall is examined. Here each leaf is of such form, size, and length of stalk that it does not seriously overlap or shut the light from any of its neighbors.

90. *Getting in the proper position.* — In addition to alterations in the form and size of the stalks and blades in order to get better exposure to light, the protoplasm has the power of moving the petiole and blade in such manner that it will receive the light in the best manner, or the one suited to its capacity. This is done by twisting or bending the stalk or petiole, or by bending the stem to which it is attached.

91. *Heliotropic movements.* — The action of the leaf or stem for placing the blades in the proper position for receiving light in response to the sensitiveness of the plant to light is termed *heliotropism.* This may be observed in house plants grown by a window. Here all of the leaves have moved in such manner as to make their blades face the window. If such a plant is turned halfway round so that the leaves face away from the window, they will quickly regain their former position. Perform this experi-

ment with a geranium, and note the position of the leaves five or six hours and a day later.

Repeat the experiment by bringing a plant from the open air and placing it in a box with one small opening. Sketch the position of the stems and leaves and do the same a day later. In what region has the movement taken place, the leaf stalk or the stem to which it is attached? The movements of roots away from the light, § 46, are to be recalled in this connection.

92. *Movements of leaves and stems in response to gravity.* — Many leaves and stems are seen to curve upward without regard to the direction from which the light comes. This power of response to gravity is termed *geotropism*. It is this property of the plant which enables it to hold its stems outright. A different kind of geotropism makes the stems of the trailing species lie along the surface of the soil

93. *Movements to avoid injury.* — The rays of light from the sun exert the greatest effect when they strike the surface of a leaf squarely or perpendicularly, as any one may know when he recalls that the sun shines the hottest when it is directly over-

head. A leaf in the open would receive the greatest amount of light if it were held in a horizontal position, and as the intensity of the light at noonday is such as to be injurious to many species, they have developed the power of changing the position of the blades at such times. This movement generally consists in tilting, so that the tip points more or less directly upward or downward. In either case the rays of the noonday sun strike the surface at such an acute angle that their effect is not so great The efficiency of this device can be very readily demonstrated if you should place one tin plate flat upon the surface of the ground, and stand another one upright on its edge, noting the difference in warmth of the two, a half hour later, by the touch. Movements of the leaves or leaflets to avoid injury from excessive light may be seen if the bean, locust, pea, or any member of the family should be examined during the warmer part of a summer day. The same plants may also move their leaves to escape dangers of another kind during chilly or cool nights.

94. *Compass plants.* — If the leaves of the wild lettuce, which is now a common weed in the United States, are examined, it will be found that those on

specimens standing out in exposed places are twisted so that they point nearly toward the north or south — a fact which has given the plant its common name. The effect of this arrangement is to present the edge of the blades to the noonday sun, and the direct rays may strike them only in mid forenoon and mid afternoon, thus avoiding the fiercer rays of the noonday sun. Only a dozen species show this interesting method of avoiding damage to the leaves.

95. *Some plants have lost the power of manufacturing chlorophyl.* — All species which take carbon dioxide from the air do so by means of the help of chlorophyl, and when they live in a place where they may get their food already formed, the green color is not needed. It is an invariable rule with all living things, that as soon as an organ or a structure or a substance becomes less useful, the succeeding generations of the plant do not perfect the useless thing. Hence the species which have become able to take up their food already formed have lost their green color. The bacteria have all done so, as well as the mushrooms, and moulds, and their relatives. A few flowering species have undergone similar changes. If a plant gets its food from the

body of another living plant or animal, it is termed a *parasite,* and a brief study has already been made of some of the characteristics of species of this kind (§ 50). If its food consists of the substance of the decaying bodies of other organisms, it is then termed a *saprophyte.* Bacteria and mushrooms and moulds offer most of the examples of both classes.

96. *An association without chlorophyl.* — It has been pointed out in a previous paragraph that some species of higher plants have fungi united with their roots, forming a partnership which is of mutual benefit. This partnership results in the seed plant securing food without making it in the usual manner, so these species lose their green color because of disuse. The leaves also decrease greatly in size, lose some of their tissues, and their characteristic position with regard to light. The Indian pipe, coral root, pine sap, and others are striking illustrations of this action.

97. *Pitchered leaves.* — Quite a large number of species have changed their leaves in such manner that they serve as traps for catching and holding animals. The bodies of these creatures are *digested* and used as food. The greatest variety is exhibited

in the method of action.   Perhaps those most easily
found and examined are the traps of the pitcher
plant (*Sarracenia*) and bladderwort (*Utricularia*).
The pitcher plant is a member of a family that
extends around the globe, and the pitchers of the
different members of the family are unlike ; the common pitcher plant, or Sarracenia, is found growing
in bogs and swamps over a large part of the United
States.   A search should be made for them in such
places, and fine specimens may be found near tama-
rac swamps.   They may be easily distinguished by
the urn-shaped leaves.   When found, note the manner in which these leaves arise in clusters from a
short underground stem.   Note the general form
and color of the organs.   Beside the green, various markings of red and purple are to be seen.
Note the following regions of the leaf : the *petiole,*
the *pitcher,* or urn-shaped part, and the *hood,* or *lip,*
at the upper outer edge.   Split a leaf from top to
bottom, noting the shape of the cavity and the contents.   What kinds of animals do you find inside ?
Next make an attempt to determine the manner
in which they were enticed or entrapped in the
pitcher.   Examine the upper and outer edge of the
pitcher for honey.   Inside and near the top of

the pitcher will be found a zone of bristly hairs, below this a smooth belt, and below this a second zone of hairs. Small animals once descending into the pitchers purposely or accidentally are unable to make their way up again through the downward pointed hairs, or across the glazed surface, and they finally fall into the liquid in the bottom of each pitcher. *Glands* on the inner surface secrete a *digestive fluid* which dissolves their bodies much like the action of a stomach, and the substances may then be absorbed. Of course not all animals are held by this trap. A winged insect very rarely escapes, however, after its wings are wet by the fluid. Beside animals, portions of twigs and leaves also fall into the pitchers and are more or less digested and absorbed by the walls. Pitchers, in addition to manufacturing food from the air by the aid of chlorophyl, are seen to gain another supply from the bodies of the entrapped animals and plants.

If convenient, the pouched leaves of the bladder-wort should be examined in the same manner. This plant floats near the surface of streams and ponds, and the traps may be seen to contain a mass of dark-colored contents which will prove to be the remains of small aquatic animals. Some species of this plant have traps large enough to receive young fishes, and they kill large numbers of these animals in the course of a season.

98. *Food-building in the lower forms.*—The leaf is the most perfect organ for the display of chlorophyl in such manner as to make the best use of light, but in lower forms it is done in a simpler manner. One generation of the mosses, ferns, and some liverworts are furnished with organs like the leaves of seed plants. In the other generation the body is in the form of a thin plate, or solid mass of cells, which lies flat on the surface of the ground. The chlorophyl in such cases is carried in the upper layers, where it may receive light. The seaweeds exhibit a great variety of organs for this purpose. Some of them are leaflike in general form, while others are massive and carry chlorophyl in the outer layers only; these plants also carry red and blue coloring matter. The pond-scums, which float on fresh water, consist of a chain of cylindrical cells, and the green color is arranged in spiral bands, like corkscrews, which run around just inside the cell wall in all cells except the spores. In still simpler forms the chlorophyl is diffused through

the whole cell and not set apart in separate bodies, as in the higher forms. Masses of pond-scum, with bubbles of oxygen attached, are easily found in almost any pond on a summer day.

99. *The leaf and water.* — All of the food taken up by the roots is dissolved in one to ten thousand times its weight of water, and is carried in this form up through the stem and out into the leaves, where it is used with the sugars to build up protoplasm or make reserve foods. Some of this great amount of water may be used also, but the greater proportion is not needed further, and since there is no method for its return to the roots it must be thrown off. This must be done principally in the form of vapor. The excretion of watery vapor constitutes the second important function of the leaf. The process is termed *transpiration*.

100. *Course of the water in the leaf.* — The water supply comes through the petiole, of course, and when it reaches the lamina it divides into numerous streams, each one of which follows a nerve or rib and goes out into all of its branches This may be demonstrated if a leaf of the maple or poplar is cut from the stem of a living tree, and the base of

G

the petiole inserted in a bottle of red ink or aniline in water. Examine a day later. The color will have marked out the *conducting system* of the leaf. This will be found to distribute the liquid to the remotest and smallest parts of the lamina.

101. *Transpiration.* — Clustered around the conducting tubes are the soft, thin-walled *mesophyl* cells, which draw water from the veins. The liquid is constantly evaporated from the walls of these cells into the air between them, and this connects with the outer air by means of the thousands of minute openings in the lower side of the leaf. The sun shines on the upper side of the leaf, heating it and the delicate cells underneath, and they constantly evaporate water into the *air spaces,* and this air laden with water pours out of the stomata and is replaced by drier air from the outside.

102. *The vapor transpired.* — That watery vapor is thrown off by the leaf may be shown if the petiole of a leaf is passed through a small hole in a large piece of cardboard and immersed in a tumbler of water. Put clay or wax around the petiole to prevent any water vapor from coming up in this way through the hole in the cardboard. Now invert a

second tumbler over the blade. Examine a few hours later. The vapor thrown off by the leaf will have collected in the form of small drops on the inside of the second tumbler.

103. *Measurement of the amount of water thrown off by a plant.* — Lay a piece of oiled cloth 18 inches square on the table, and in the centre set a potted geranium or tomato. Bring the edges of the cloth up around the pot and tie closely around the base of the stem. Water can now evaporate from the plant only. Set on one pan of a grocer's scale and place weights in the other pan until it balances.

If a scale is not to be had, suspend a wooden rod by the middle and to each end tie a small bucket. Place the plant in one and weights in the other. Examine a few hours later. The plant will have grown lighter. Remove weights from the opposite end of the beam until the balance is restored. How much weight has been taken out? This represents the amount of the water thrown off by the plant.

104. *Sunlight increases transpiration.* — Repeat this experiment in the sunlight and compare the amount of water lost with that of the previous experience.

105. *Regulation and control of transpiration.* — The leaf is able to control the amount of water given off by opening and closing the stomata. The amount of moisture already in the air influences the transpiration greatly, and as this amount varies widely in different places there are a large number of forms of leaves adapted to the different conditions. The leaf may shield itself from the drying effects of intense sunlight by heavy *cuticles, coats of hair,* or *wax,* or by the upright positions described in § 93.

106. *Wax or bloom as a means of prevention of excessive loss of water.* — Select some leaf which has the surfaces covered with a *whitish bloom* (cabbage). Rub the bloom from one and place it by the side of a second which has been handled carefully in order not to disturb the bloom. Which is the more wilted in two or three hours ? The best results will be obtained if the leaves are placed in the sunlight.

107. *Size of leaves and dryness of the air.* — Species growing in dry air generally exhibit very small leaves, while those living in wet places or where the air is very damp develop large laminæ. It is necessary to have a stream of water constantly travelling from the roots to the leaves, and plants living in

very damp or rainy situations secure this stream by building very large leaves. The banana is a common example, and many other tropical plants show leaves several times as large.

108. *Sleep movements.* — If the position of the leaflets of the bean or locust are noticed at sunset or later, it will be seen that their blades are placed nearly vertically. This position is supposed to be a method of preventing the leaf from cooling so rapidly as it would if held horizontal, and also from accumulating a layer of dew which would hinder transpiration. (See also § 93.)

109. *Velvety surfaces.* — If the leaves of some of the species of begonias are examined, they will be found to show an upper surface that is velvety to the touch, and when examined with a hand lens appear to have an immense number of small projections. This is due to the fact that the cells of the upper side of the leaf are all extended in little *cones*. The cones entrap the rays of sunlight as it were, and refract them so that they warm the leaf and increase the transpiration over what it would be if the surface were smooth. This device is also exhibited by the *petals* of violets, pansies, and primulas.

110. *Autumnal leaf fall.* — The greater number of the hardy or long-lived plants of the United States are *deciduous*, or drop their leaves every year. This casting of the leaves is one of the distinctive features of the close of the growing season. It is popularly supposed to be due to the action of cold, but this is a mistake. The leaves of a large tree throw off as much as a barrel of water in the course of a day, and when the plant finds that it is losing water in the dry August days faster than it can take it up from the soil, it begins to get rid of the organs which use most of it.

111. *Separatory layer.* — In order to be able to cut off the leaf quickly and economically, a ring of tissue is formed at the base of the stalk, which spreads the other tissues apart as it grows. After this *separating layer* is fully formed it is very brittle, and the slightest breath of wind will split it apart and allow the leaf to fall to the ground. In compound leaves, such as the horse-chestnut, separatory layers are formed at the base of each leaflet also, and in some ivies a piece of the branch is cut off with the leaf.

If a twig of maple with the attached leaf is taken

from the tree in September, and a slicing cut is made through the base of the petiole and the twig, the separatory layer may then be seen with a magnifying glass. Trees which usually shed their leaves are sometimes seen to retain them during the winter. This is usually due to the fact that the formation of the separatory layer has been interrupted by cold or drought.

112. *The length of life of leaves.* — The leaves of the conifers and other *evergreen* trees may remain in place on the branches two or three years, or even longer. After a time, however, they become damaged by the wind, and by insects or other agencies, and are cast off. An evergreen tree is casting its leaves almost continually, but as it loses but a few at a time it is not noticeable. Quite a deep layer of needles may be found underneath almost any pine tree.

113. *Growth of leaves.* — The greatest variation is shown in the method and rapidity of growth. All parts of the organ do not grow with equal rapidity, as may be seen by the following test: Mark off intervals with India ink on the petioles and midribs of leaves of sunflowers, narcissus, and any other con-

venient species. Measure from day to day and find
the total increase in length, and note the region of
greatest growth. In general, it will be found that
grasslike leaves grow at the base, while others
extend chiefly by the development of the terminal
portion.

114. *Wilting.* — If the leaf of any rapidly growing
plant is taken off and laid in the sun for an hour,
it may be seen that it becomes limp and is said to be
wilted. Compare with a fresh leaf. It is quite flexible, and the soft tissues between the ribs appear to
be shrunken. Hold an end of the leaf in either hand
and pull until it breaks in two parts. Repeat with
a fresh leaf. The wilted leaf is as strong in this
way as the fresh one. It has not lost any of its
mechanical tissues, and its limpness must be due to
the loss of water. The cells of fresh leaves of the
plant are filled with water to such extent that
they are stretched and the walls are very firm, in
the same manner that the string of a bow is as rigid
as a bar of iron when the bow is prepared for use,
but quite limp and flexible when separate.

At noonday in midsummer and at other times the
leaves do not receive as much water as they evapo-

rate, and as a consequence they wilt more or less. The wilting is itself a protection against serious injury, for in this condition the openings on the lower surface of the leaf are closed, and the drooping position assumed by the blade operates to diminish the amount of water thrown off into the air.

115. *Transplanting trees and herbs is attended by wilting.*—A plant usually develops a system of roots with hairs capable of supplying the necessary amount of moisture to the leaves, and when it is lifted from the ground the process is attended with more or less damage to the roots or hairs. When the plant is set in a new position its absorbing powers are not so great as before, and if it is allowed to retain all of its leaves, it will throw off more water than it receives, and wilting will result. To avoid this the branches are trimmed in such manner as to reduce the evaporating surface to the proper proportion to the roots. One may see nurserymen putting out trees, the tops of which have been trimmed to bare poles.

116. *Freezing or frosting.*—An observation of the plants growing in the open air after the first frost of autumn will show that the leaves of some

species are quite blackened and shrivelled, while others still appear bright and green and remain so until the actual approach of winter and many frosts have been endured. This leads at once to the conclusion that separate species have different powers of resistance to cold.

It is seen at once that a temperature sufficient to freeze water does not kill all species. Then again some species, such as the melons, coleus, tobacco, and tropical plants are killed by temperatures of two degrees above the freezing point. Apple leaves are killed by a temperature of two to six degrees below the freezing point, cabbage five to seventeen below, peaches two or three below, tomatoes one below, wheat one below, strawberries two to four below, while the grasses of the Arctic regions endure temperatures of eighty and ninety below the freezing point.

The water in some species may be frozen without damage to the protoplasm, but if the frozen specimens are brought into a warm room and thawed quickly, the shock of the sudden change will kill them. It is for this reason that frozen specimens may be sometimes thawed without damage in water. The use of the water also prevents the specimen from drying out.

117. *The air is colder on a frosty night near the ground than it is a few feet above it.* — If one thermometer is hung near the surface of the ground on a quiet night in mid autumn, and another ten to twenty-five feet higher in the branches of a tree, it will be found that it may be five to ten degrees colder near the ground than it is in the tree tops. This is due to the fact that the soil cools very rapidly, and the layer of air resting on it is also cooled, while the upper air is comparatively warm. On account of this fact the leaves and buds on the lower branches of a tree may be frosted, while those on the upper part are untouched. The low-growing shrubs and herbs will be frosted before the taller trees. If, however, a great movement of wind from the northward covers the country with cold air, it will result in a general freeze which affects all alike. The farmer and the fruit raiser prevent damage to their crops from frosts by covering the plants with a shield which will prevent the loss of heat by the ground and by the plants, by building fires to heat up the layer of cold air, or by making smudge fires which add heat, smoke, and moisture to the air, making a fog blanket that prevents the loss of heat as effectually as a covering of cloth might do it.

None of these devices may protect against freezing in general cold weather.

118. *Drainage of cold air.* — The layer of cold air on the surface of the soil is heavier than the warm air above it, and in rough or broken country this heavier air flows down hill as water would, accumulating in the valleys, which thus become very much colder than the hill-tops around them. The temperature of the valleys is often ten to twenty degrees lower than that of the hills near by. As a consequence of this fact, vineyards, orchards, and gardens, in which delicate varieties are cultivated, are planted on ridges and hills in preference to low-lying valleys.

VI. STEMS

119. *The nature of stems.* — The stem is the *main axis,* or central member of the body of the plant. From its lower end the roots arise and penetrate the soil, while leaves and reproductive organs are borne on its upper part. Stems are often described as springing from roots, when they grow from underground stems. This is a mistake, except in a very few instances in which roots are capable of giving rise to stems.

It is necessary that the roots should be buried in the soil for the purpose of absorbing food, and that the leaves should be held up in the sunlight to enable them to form food; also that the reproductive organs should be held in a position that will enable them to perpetuate the species. This means that the roots on one hand and the leaves and flowers on the other may be separated by some distance. The stem is the connecting member, and its bulk and length will vary with the habits and needs of the separate species.

120. *Stems are made up of sections, or internodes.*
— If the stem of a mint or of the corn is examined,
it will be found that it exhibits a number of
" joints," indicated by external ridges which divide
it into a number of sections. Take two sections of
the stem not adjoining, and compare them. No difference will be found except in the matter of size
and age. The arrangement of the tissues is identical. Repetition of this test will show that a stem is
made up of a number of sections of the same structure. This characteristic is one which is not found
in any other member of the plant.

121. *Branches arise at the nodes or joints only.*
— The branches of roots were seen to arise at
any point on the main root. Leaves, branches,
and flowers are seen to be given off at the
nodes only of stems. Roots emerge from the extreme lower end of the stem, or they may arise
from the lower nodes, as in the case of the stilt or
prop roots of the corn, or from any part of the stem
in climbing species.

122. *Relation of the leaves and branches.* — It
may be seen that buds or branches arise from the
stem immediately above the point at which a petiole

is attached, that is, in the *axil* of the leaf. While this is generally the case, yet many species give off branches just below the leaf. Wherever a branch is seen on a stem, one may be certain that it arose originally just above or below a leaf. The leaf has fallen off, and the branch has continued to grow and enlarge until all trace of the leaf is lost.

123. *Leaf traces.* — When the leaf falls from the stem its petiole is cut off cleanly by means of the separatory layer described in a previous paragraph. The *scar* is noticeable for some time, and may be seen very plainly on the twigs of the maple, oak, or chestnut, or on the vine of the grape.

124. *Relation of leaves and flowers.* — Flower stalks are also seen to arise from the axils of leaves. A single flower on its own stalk may arise from the axil of the leaf without changing the character or the size of the latter in any way. When a branch bears a great number of flowers closely crowded together, like the lobelia, the mints, mullein, and larkspur, the leaves at the basis of the numerous flower stalks are much smaller than those on other parts of the stem, and are scarcely more than little wedges of green tissue which are termed *bracts*.

125. *Structure of stems.* — If a small branch of the elm, beech, maple, or chestnut is cut off and then a portion of the branch is split lengthwise, it may be seen that a hard covering of bark encloses the whole. Immediately inside this is a layer of soft tissue of material easily crushed and full of water. This material is living while the bark was chiefly made up of dead tissues. Small extensions of the living tissue penetrate the wood which occupies the greater part of the volume of the branch. In the centre is to be seen a small amount of soft *pith*, which may easily be cut or torn, and is generally made up of dead cells in older branches. The branch is thus seen to be composed of living and dead cells, and the dead tissue greatly exceeds the living in bulk.

126. *Uses of stems.* — The purpose of the stem is twofold : to hold up the leaves and flowers, and to conduct water and food between the leaves and roots. The method by which these functions are carried out may be best understood after a study of the scheme in which the tissues are arranged in the stem. This has been seen roughly in the branch of the tree examined, but it will be necessary to see the manner in which the different parts of the living

and dead tissues are disposed with regard to each other.

127. *Methods by which firmness is secured.* — If the stem is to hold the leaves and flowers aloft, it must secure a certain amount of rigidity in its own body. It does this by two methods, which may be illustrated as follows : Cut off a fresh branch from a woody tree, and also the stem of a tomato or potato, and lay in the hot sun for two hours. Take a second fresh branch from the tree and bend or break it across the knee. Bend or break the one which has lain in the sun in the same manner. Has the latter lost any of its rigidity or firmness? Is it more easily bent? Repeat with other stems. What is the result? It will doubtless be found that the *herbaceous* stem has lost its firmness and that it is wilted and may be very easily bent double, while the *woody* stem is practically unchanged. Both stems lost water in the sun. This did not affect the woody stem, but did the other. It seems fair to conclude that the presence of water is necessary for the firmness of herbaceous stems, and it is not for the woody stems. If the experiment is carried farther, it will be found that dead and thoroughly dried stems

H

are more rigid than the living members. This is due to the fact that even the soft living tissues become hard when dead and dry.

Stems secure firmness by the presence of hard mechanical tissues and by filling soft tissues full of water under pressure, as in leaves.

128. *Arrangement of hard or dead cells to secure firmness of stems.* — The dead cells of stems are arranged in the form of strands or girders after the principles used by an engineer or architect in constructing a tower or tall building. The architect uses wood, brick, cement, and metal as material from which to construct the tower. The plant uses *wood, bast,* which resembles cable or wire rope in its properties and is as strong as wrought-iron, *collenchyma,* which is elastic, and also soft *pith* cells. The properties of wood are too well known to need discussion. Bast cells make up the fibres which are taken from the flax plant and used by man, and collenchyma forms the sharp angles of the stems of the mints and is very much like cartilage or rubber. The plant has thus rigid beams, flexible cables, and soft spongelike filling or cement for its building materials, and the towers it constructs are greater in

height in proportion to thickness, and show greater strength and efficiency, than those built by man.

129. *Arrangement of mechanical tissues in a stem of a grass.* — Secure an uninjured cornstalk. Take out a single internode, or the part between two joints, and dissect it. Note the hard plates which extend entirely through the stem at the nodes. The outer layer is in the form of a cylinder and is hard and rigid. Cut in two parts lengthwise. The interior is filled with the soft pith. In this pith are great numbers of strands and fibres which run from the plate at one end to the other. Now split the entire piece into small strips, and without injuring any of the separate parts tie them together in a bundle. Lay the bundle on a table with half of its length projecting over the edge. Weight down the end on the table. Now tie weights to the other end and determine the amount necessary to break the bundle of building material. Repeat the operation with a section of the stem which has not been dissected. It will doubtless be seen that the materials themselves are not very strong, but when fitted together in proper form they make an extremely rigid stem.

The cornstalk is seen to be a cylindrical tower, many storeys in height. Each storey is filled with the cementing pith, and numerous braces run from the ceiling to the floor of each in a method that could not be improved by the best engineer.

130. *Mechanical tissues in a sunflower stem.* — Repeat the above experiment with the stem of the sunflower. Cut across a young stem and note the position of the building elements. A few strands of wood will be found arranged in a circle, and on the outer side of each bundle of wood is a bundle of bast. The centre of the stem is filled with pith.

131. *Mechanical tissues in a carnation stem.* — Repeat the tests of strength with a carnation stem. Cut a stem length- and cross-wise and note the manner in which the material is arranged. The bast will be found to form a circle, and immediately attached to the inside of this circle is a second circle of wood. The centre is filled with pith. This stem is then like a tower made of two strong tubes fastened together, and the centre is filled with the cementing pith, which is also living and which becomes firm and bracing by the absorption of water. Examine the stem of a mint in the same manner.

132. *Arrangement of mechanical tissues in a petiole.* — The types of stems described above stand erect and support the weight of the leaves like a pillar, and the bending force of the wind like a tower. The petioles of leaves generally hold the blade in a horizontal position, and the weight acts always to bend the petiole in one direction, downward. To meet this strain it is necessary to have the building material arranged in a half circle, as may be seen if the leaf of the maple or chestnut is examined.

133. *The firmness of plants that become limp when dried.* — Select a young stem of any plant which would become limp if you laid it in the sun. The tips of elder stems in April or May will offer splendid material. Cut away from opposite sides of the stem until only a thin strip remains, which includes the central part of the stem. Now divide this exactly down the middle with a sharp knife. This will make two sheets of material, each of which is composed of a strip of living pith full of water under pressure, and the wood which will bend but not stretch. After a few minutes place the two strips together in their original position. What changes

of form have they undergone? Cut the stalks of the calla lily or rhubarb into strips, and note behavior.

134. *Stems as conducting organs.* — The position of the stem between the leaves where sugars and other substances are manufactured and the roots where water and mineral salts are taken up makes it necessary for it to conduct the products of the leaf downward, and the materials taken up by the leaf upward. There is a stream of water upward and a stream of food material downward, but the two are not connected, and there is nothing like a circulation of the sap.

135. *Upward path of sap.* — Cut off a stem of the tomato or touch-me-not with a number of sound leaves attached, and thrust the lower end of the stem into a bottle of red ink or a tumbler of water colored with aniline dye. After four or five hours remove and dissect the stem. What portions are colored? This will show through what tissues the liquid has passed. It is to be seen that the dead wood cells also serve as conduits for water in addition to their function of making the stem rigid.

136. *Path of sap in large trees.* — Each year a new layer of wood is added to the trunk of a tree, thus increasing its thickness by the small part of an inch. If the previous experiment might be repeated with a large tree, it would be found that only the outer layers of wood in the trunk would be colored, showing that it is through these only that the sap ascends.

137. *Girdling.* — An interesting fact in this connection is the behavior of a tree when girdled. Girdling is usually done by removing the bark, the living layer, and some of the outer wood of the trunk, and is done for the purpose of killing the tree. In most species the removal of the outer layer of wood cuts off the conduits which carry the water to the leaves, and if it is done in the spring, the tree generally dies the following summer. Some are able to send water up through the inner layers, and not only live that year but the following year also. A few instances have been found in which the tree has survived the operation many years.

138. *Downward path of material from the leaf.* — Trees which live through one summer but die at the beginning of the next, are injured by starvation of

the roots.   These organs are constantly receiving material from the leaves, but have a surplus on hand almost all of the time, and some is also to be found in the lower part of the stem.   During the first year this is sufficient for their nourishment, but it is generally exhausted before the beginning of the next season.   This material passes down very slowly through the layer of living tissue immediately underneath the bark, and its flow is interrupted in any girdling operation.   If the tree lives several years after girdling, it may be supposed that its roots have formed partnership with fungi in such manner that it receives its food from them (see § 52).   As a matter of fact the stumps of many of the coniferous trees are known to live for long periods, perhaps a decade, by means of food obtained in this manner.

Girdling of branches is used as a method of increasing the size and quality of fruit borne on them.

139. *Forces which carry the sap upward through the stem.* — Information upon the forces which pump water up to the top of tall trees is very incomplete. It is quite certain that it needs as much power to carry water to the top of a tree a hundred feet high

as it does to send it up through an iron pipe to the same distance. As a matter of fact it takes more force to carry it up in the tree because it must pass through such very small vessels. While the whole process may not be fully understood, yet some features of it may be illustrated in the following paragraphs.

140. *Root or bleeding pressure.* — If the stump of a tree which has been cut down in the spring is examined it will be seen that the sap is oozing from the cut surface in great volume, and if a cup is placed under the cut end of a grapevine at this season the amount of liquid thrown out may be measured. This *bleeding* is due to a pressure exerted by the living cells of the stem and roots, and it is sufficient to force water to the tops of small plants like the sunflower in the temperate zone and in trees in the tropics, but in the United States it could not send sap to the leaves of large trees. Then, again, root pressure is strong only in early spring.

141. *The flow of sap of the sugar maple.* — Not all flow of sap is due to bleeding pressure. Sugar maples are tapped to obtain the sweet sap at a time in the spring when the ground is still frozen. The

flow is due in part to the effect of the sun's rays upon the trunk, heating and expanding the liquids and gases in it, and driving the sap out the auger hole in this way. After the ground thaws out the sap ceases to flow in quantity.

The sugar obtained from the sap has been stored up in the pith cells in the rays of the wood during the winter.

142. *Dew.* — The sparkling gems of dew which make a lawn so beautiful of a summer morning are not usually formed from the air, but are drops of water which have been forced up through the leaves by the root pressure. During the warm and sunny part of the day the water is thrown off by the leaf as fast as it may be received from the roots, but at night the air is cool and moist, and it is not able to do so. As a consequence, the liquid is forced up until it fills the spaces in the leaf and finally oozes out through slits in the epidermis. Of course dew may be formed by the condensation of moisture from the atmosphere, but that on grass usually comes up from the roots.

143. *How to cause a plant to form dew at any time.* — By putting a plant in the same conditions as

the grass at night, it can be induced to form dew. To do this, set a large glass dish over a vigorous plant of geranium or begonia in such manner that it will be tightly enclosed. If it remains in this position for a few hours, the air inside the vessel becomes saturated with watery vapor, and the leaves are unable to throw off any more. The continued supply from the roots is forced out through the leaf at the edges in the form of large drops. These become so large that they fall off and others collect in the same place, so that moist spots will be formed in the soil where they fall. This demonstration will be most successful if the plant is allowed to remain covered over night.

144. *Lifting power of leaves and branches.* — It has been shown in a previous experiment (§ 135) that a leafy stem will pull colored fluid upward in the stem, and if proper apparatus were at hand it could be proved that it does so with great force. Both the lifting power of the leaves, and the pumping power of the roots seem insufficient to send up the necessary amount of water to the leaves, for it will be remembered that a poplar tree uses a barrel or more of water every day during the summer,

and smaller quantities at other times. There is still much to be found out about the ascent of sap.

145. *Growth of stems.* — The manner in which stems grow and increase in size bears a close relation to the arrangement of the mechanical elements. The arrangement of the living tissues is different in the various types, of course. From the many forms of the stem it will be most profitable to select a tree and the cornstalk for study of this feature.

146. *Action of embryonic tissue of a tree.* — The living cells of a tree which constantly divide, forming others which pass into dead tissue, lie immediately underneath the bark and completely sheathe the trunk, forming a small cone of delicate cells at the tips of the stems and branches and in the buds. Dead cells are constantly being formed on the inner side of this layer and added to the wood. The cells formed in any one season are distinguishable from those of the last season and constitute an *annual ring*, though sometimes two rings may be formed in one summer. At the same time dead cells are being added to the bark on the outer side of the living tissue. The living cells at the

tip divide and push forward, leaving dead cells behind them.

147. *Growth in length and diameter.*—Dead cells do not increase in size, of course, so that the trunk of a tree does not elongate except at the tips of the stems and branches. Thus a branch on the trunk will always remain the same distance from the roots. Its distance from the ground might be increased by the washing away of the soil below it. This may be demonstrated if a nail is driven in the trunk of a tree near the surface of the soil, and a second as high above it as may be convenient. Measure the distance between them quite exactly, and then repeat a few months or a year later.

148. *Measurement of growth in length.*—Mark the stem of some rapidly growing plant, such as bean or sunflower, with India-ink at intervals of half an inch. Measure these intervals on three or more successive days. Do all of them increase? What part of the stem increases in length with greatest rapidity?

149. *Measurement of growth in diameter.*—The increase in diameter of a plant is not so easily

obtained. Perhaps the best method is to drive two nails into the opposite sides of the trunk of a vigorous young poplar in early spring, and then find the exact circumference of the tree an inch above these nails with a tape measure. Repeat the operation of measurement about the first of September.

150. *The bark.* — The behavior of bark should be studied in connection with growth in thickness. The young poplar and many other young trees are seen to have a smooth bark, while older specimens have a very rough or even a shaggy covering. The cells which compose the bark of the younger trees are alive, and divide and grow in such manner that they keep pace with the increase of the trunk. After the tree reaches a certain age the bark does this no longer. Any increase in the trunk then results in the splitting of the bark, leaving the edges exposed. A new layer of bark is formed which is applied to the inside of this slit like a patch. This process is repeated every year, and as a consequence some trees, such as the oaks, hickories, and poplars, have a very rough or shaggy bark. The sycamore is an example of a tree which casts away the old layer of bark each year and

presents a new coat of smooth, clean, greenish white bark to the weather. The bark serves to protect the layer of living tissue from damage by the climate, or by animals, or from the falling trunks or branches of other trees. On the other hand, the numerous crevices afford lodgment and refuge for the spores of parasitic fungi which germinate and injure the tree, and also harbors insects and other animals which work injury in many ways.

151. *Growth of a corn stem.* — Select a young and rapidly growing corn stem and mark off three or four of the terminal internodes into half-inch intervals by means of India-ink. Measure these from day to day for a week. What places show elongation ?

Trees are generally larger at the bases, but in the corn plant and in the palms and their relatives the basal part of the stem will be found to be smaller than parts of the stem above it. This is due to the fact that such stems soon reach their full growth in thickness at the base, and the later portions formed may receive more food and attain a greater thickness.

152. *Nodding or circular movements due to unequal growth.* — Select a vigorous specimen of the hop, bean, or morning-glory, and tie all of it to an upright stake except the tip of the stem a foot in length. Now set a second thin stake in the ground so that its top is just below the tip of the stem. Note the position of the tip an hour later. If it has moved, set up another stake. Repeat this process until the tip has moved around in a complete circle. What was the direction of the movement? What length of time was necessary to complete the circle? This circular movement of the tip is due to the fact that one side of the stem grows faster than the other sides for a short time, then it slows down and a region next to it grows most rapidly, and so on around the stem. This results in tilting the tip toward every point of the compass in succession.

A nodding movement, due to the alternate growth of two sides of a flattened organ, may be seen if the growing leaves of narcissus are observed in this manner.

153. *Length of life.* — The length of time a single specimen of a plant may live varies enor-

mously. Thus in some of the lower forms an individual may be grown from a spore, attain maturity, give rise to new individuals, and die in a few hours or even in a few minutes. The spores of these same species may be capable of living many years in a resting condition, however. Among the seed plants the cycle of life varies from sixty or seventy days in some of the herbs to three thousand years in certain kinds of trees. It is estimated that some trees can live to twice this age, though the lack of records does not allow this to be verified. The estimation of the age of a tree by counting the annual rings is subject to error, since the number of these rings may be nearly twice the age of the tree in years. All seed plants may be roughly classed as *annuals, biennials,* and *perennials.*

154. *Annuals.* — Annuals are those which live but one season. The seeds germinate, and a system of roots, a stem, and branches are formed, and seeds are matured in a period which varies from two to four months. Species of this character may generally be distinguished by the character of the stem and root system. Annuals live through the winter in the form of seeds only. Examine twenty species

I

and select the annuals. What cultivated plants are grown as annuals?

155. *Biennials.* — A second group of species germinate the seeds, form a stem with a rosette of leaves and an extensive root system in one year, and then develop the flower-bearing branches, flowers, and seeds the second season. Some of the thistles and the common mullein belong to this class.

156. *Perennials.* — Quite a large number of species germinate the seeds and form stems the first year, then rest during the winter, and continue growth during the next season and for many successive seasons. In trees and similar forms the entire stem remains alive, and consequently it increases in bulk each year, attaining an enormous size. The giant trees of California have attained a trunk about four hundred and fifty feet high, and thirty feet in diameter. These are by no means the tallest trees in the world.

Another class of perennials have a stem which lies just underneath the surface of the soil, sending branches up into the air each year. These die down on the approach of winter. Meanwhile the underground stem grows at the tip, and would increase its length, but the other end of the stem, which is also the oldest, constantly dies away so that the plant does not greatly increase in size. The great size of the bulky perennials subjects them to many dangers which the underground stem does not incur, and it would be difficult to set a limit to the age which the latter may reach. The ravages of animals, extremes of heat and cold, washing away of the soil by rains, or the growth of more vigorous species around them, would tend to set a limit to the age which they may attain.

157. *Changes in the length of life of a species.* — The length of life of any species is an adaptation to the conditions under which it lives. Changes may be brought about when the plant is introduced into a new *habitat*. Thus the ordinary tomato is an annual, as it is grown in gardens; yet if it is cultivated in a greenhouse and sheltered from the weather, it may live two or three times as long. Bringing a species into a severer climate may have the effect of reducing a perennial or a biennial to an annual.

158. *Buds* — Immediately underneath the epidermis, or bark, lies the layer of living tissue which is

capable of great multiplication of cells and growth. At certain points this tissue has acquired the power of forming new branches, flowers, and leaves, hence it is called embryonic tissue. These specialized masses of cells are generally in the form of minute outgrowths, and are located at the tips of the stem and its branches as well as in the axils of the leaves. This tissue is most delicate and easily injured, and is generally protected by coverings of leaves or bracts. The growing points or masses of embryonic cells and their coverings form *buds*.

159. *Naked buds.*—In species growing in tropical and mild climates the buds are only slightly shielded by the young leaves near the tip of the stem, and no special coverings are developed. Such an arrangement is called a *naked bud*, and an example may be seen in the cultivated geranium or pelargonium.

160. *Scaly buds.*—Plants which grow in cold or dry climates generally adopt some method of protecting the growing points from damage. The most common device is a number of wrappings of brownish *scales*, which are in reality a special form of leaves which are used for protection instead of

food formation. The scales are fitted around the growing point so closely as to make a compact conical mass that is very firm. In addition the scales are often furnished with a coat of hairs or a layer of balsam or varnish which makes them absolutely waterproof. These scales do not keep the growing plant warmer than the surrounding air, but they protect it from damage by ice or frost, and also prevent drying out.

161. *Buds of the apple.*—Secure some winter buds of the apple by cutting off twigs two feet in length two weeks before the subject is to be studied, and placing the cut ends of the stems in a dish of water in a warm room. Now carefully dissect some buds freshly procured from the tree. Take off the scales, one at a time, noting the manner in which they are fitted to each other. The central mass of the bud should contain the young leaves and perhaps flowers. Tear apart and note shape and size. Later examine the opening buds. What changes have taken place which would cause the scales to come apart? and what changes have occurred in the shape and size of the leaves and flowers? Note all these points by sketches.

162. *Buds of elder, maple, or elm.*—Sketch a twig of one of these plants, showing the leaf scars and the position and size of the buds. Treat as above.

163. *Sleeping buds.*—It is to be seen that a bud is simply a young branch, and, furthermore, that all the branches of the plant are developed in this manner. It is important, therefore, that the plant should be furnished with an ample supply of them, so that the destruction of a few need not deprive it entirely of the power of making new branches. There is one or perhaps more of these growing points at the base of every leaf. Only a small proportion of them develop in any year, the remainder lying quiescent, and may continue to do so for years, being known as *sleeping buds.* Many of these structures may be found on the lower parts of the stems of young trees.

164. *The awakening of sleeping buds.*—If the top of a tree is cut off, some of the sleeping buds remaining on the upper part of the stem start into life, developing branches, and giving the plant a low, compact appearance. In the pruning

of fruit trees the sleeping buds are often called into action.

165. *Winter buds of aquatic plants.* — In one class of land plants the upper branches of the stem have been seen to die down, leaving only the basal portion of the stem with its buds to live through the winter. Exactly the reverse action takes place in some aquatic plants which root in the bottom of streams or lakes, or which float on the surface. If a visit is made to a lake or pond about the time that the trees have lost all their leaves, this curious bud formation may be found. The stems of the pond-weeds, stonewort, bladderwort, and others will be seen to have taken on a brownish color except at the tips. Here the stem is still alive, and a large number of leaves of a dark green color overlap each other closely, forming an egg-shaped mucilaginous mass. Break off some of these buds and find if they will float alone. These buds are sometimes termed *hibernacula.* Preserve your notes upon the subject and visit the same pond in the following spring as soon as the ice has melted. A great number of the winter buds may be seen floating near the surface of the water. Examine, and note their

Missing Page

167 *Bulbs.* — Split an onion, hyacinth bulb, or any similar structure. It will be seen that it is simply a great bud, with the scales which surround the growing point very much thickened and loaded with food. The centre of the bud is a short, thickened stem. *Bulbs* are buds that are usually detached from the plant as soon as they are formed, and when they grow, they as well as hibernacula make a new individual and therefore serve to reproduce the species (§ 183).

168. *Corms* — An interesting method by which delicate plants endure a severe winter consists in the formation of short, thick, upright stems, like those of the calla or the jack-in-the-pulpit. Examples of the latter may be found in almost any woods. On the upper side of such short squat stems may be found a large conical bud, covered by a few large scales, wrapped tightly around the central mass. Cut open such a bud; the young leaves and flowers for the next season will be found perfectly formed, except in size, as early as June or July, ten months before they are to be called into action.

169. *Forcing, or inducing an earlier growth.* — If these corms are taken from the soil in the autumn

and allowed to remain out of doors in the cold until the first of December, then put in a cellar for a month or two, they may then be potted and will begin to grow. Note the behavior of the bud covering. It does not burst open immediately, but elongates until it reaches the surface of the soil, and then only does it open and expose the young leaves. Set the pot with the growing bud in a dark room, or cover it with a pile of moss. The bud will continue to elongate until it reaches the light, or it has attained a length of seven or eight inches, which seems to be its limit of growth. Its purpose is to bring the leaves above the surface of the ground, and it does not open until it is struck by the light, which is usually a signal that this has been accomplished.

170. *Some protective devices of the shoot.* — Leaves and stems are subject to destruction by animals which use them for food, and a large number of species are furnished with structures which hinder or prevent attack by the animal. The most common means of protection consists in *poisonous* or *bitter* substances in the tissues, *spines, prickles, bristles, thorns,* and *stinging hairs.*

The acrid burning sensation which follows tasting

jack-in-the-pulpit preserves it from the ravages of grazing animals, and the well-known qualities of the poison ivies serve a similar purpose. The active substance in the latter case is an oil secreted by the leaves and stems, making even proximity dangerous to the animal.

The prickles of roses and other shrubs are examples of weapons coming from the epidermis of the stems, and which may come away in the body of the animal which comes into contact with the stems. The thorns of many species, including the well-known honey locust (*Gleditschia*), are branches which have altered their method of growth in such manner that they are very effective weapons for defence.

The edges of the leaves of some grasses are cut into saw teeth, and these are edged with *silica* so finely that they cut the flesh like knives. The margins and surfaces of thistle leaves and stems are drawn out into spines, the protective value of which may be easily seen.

The members of the cactus family protect their bodies to a great extent by sharp spines, many of which are *barbed*. These spines are modified leaves which have lost the original function of such organs, and have become solely organs of defence.

Animals, on the other hand, are constantly striving to use the bodies of these plants for food without injury from their weapons, and some of them succeed even with such well-protected forms as the cactus and the thistle. Some grazing animals may even eat poison ivy without harm.

171. *Branches used as leaves.* — A species may find itself in a location to which its leaves are wholly unsuited, and it may cease to develop these organs in the usual way. In such instances branches are sometimes modified to carry on the work that should be done by the leaf. An example of this may be seen in the " smilax " of the gardener, which is used so profusely for decorative purposes. The slender, thin bodies having the appearance of leaves are really short branches, and the true leaves are to be found as small colorless or brownish bracts at the lower side of the base of these leaflike branches.

172. *The part of stems in the struggle for existence.* — If the surface of the earth were level and plain, and the number of plants were not so great as to fully occupy this space, probably all species would form short stems which would simply lift the leaves and flowers from the ground.

The number of individuals which attempt to grow on any given spot, however, is many times greater than it can support. The species which are capable of sending up long stems quickly will reach the sunlight and live while their slower and weaker neighbors will be choked or shaded out. In this fight the stem is the chief weapon.

173. *Weeds.* — In the cultivation of crop plants all species are killed by the farmer except the one desired, thus removing it from the struggle for existence with neighbors. Certain forms, however, have habits of growth which adapt them for gaining a foothold among the cultivated forms, and this makes them weeds. Before the country was settled or cultivated there were no weeds, of course. Vigorous and rapid growth of the stems is the principal characteristic of weeds. The stems do not always stand erect, but may carpet the soil and hinder the growth of other plants in this manner. Find and describe the habits of three weeds.

174. *Climbing stems.* — In the struggle to get the leaves and flowers up to the sunlight, a number of species have formed the habit of clinging to the stems of other plants. This is done by two methods:

the stem of the climber may coil or twine around the body of the supporting plant, or it may attach itself by means of roots or tendrils.

The hop and morning-glory are examples of the twiners, and the circular movement of the tips of the stems is one of the factors in coiling it round the support. Examine one of these plants, or a bean vine, and note the firmness with which it is attached.

That plants climb by means of roots has already been noticed (§ 28). The most effective climbing devices, however, are *tendrils*. These are generally modified stems, branches, flower stalks, or even leaves.

Examine the tendrils of a squash, pumpkin, passion flower, or balsam apple (*Micrampelis*). They will be seen to be long slender bodies arising at the nodes of the stem at the bases of the leaves. Observe their movement in the same manner as in the stems (§ 152). The tendril appears to be curved, with a hooked tip. Draw its exact outline. Now rub the surface on the inner side of the curve with a pencil, and look for changes in form. It curves at the place touched. Take note of the time and extent of the movement. If the pencil were held in place, the tendril would coil around it. Look for instances of tendrils which have just formed a coil around a support. Now observe the older tendrils toward the base of the stem. What other action has the tendril shown beside coiling around the support? The formation of the spiral coils shortens the tendril and brings the stem nearer the support. Thus as the tip of the stem elongates these organs are formed at each node, and they revolve in the air until coming in contact with a support: quickly coiling round this, the free portion of the organ is thrown into a coil lifting up the stem a distance of a few inches. The force exerted in the lifting would raise a weight of one to three ounces, which is much more than the weight of the stem to which the tendril is attached. Compare the action of the tendrils of three species. After the body of the plant has been fastened to the support by means of the tendrils, the coiled portions act as springs in resisting the action of the wind or any other force which would tend to tear the plant from its support. Test this by hand.

175. *The irritability or sensitiveness of stems.* — It has been shown in a previous paragraph (§ 91) that the light which shines on the leaf may send an impulse to the stem to which it is attached, causing a

curvature which will place the leaf in the most advantageous position for the performance of its work. The stem is sensitive to light itself, as may be shown if a specimen stripped of leaves is placed near a window, when it can be seen to bend toward the light.

176. *Sensitiveness to gravity.*—Select a vigorously growing specimen of a tomato planted in a pot, and place it with the stem in a horizontal position. Observe the stem a day later. In what region has the curvature taken place? Repeat this experiment with a grass. Note the stems of plants in the woods and meadows which have been thrown down by the wind or other causes, and the tips have curved in response to gravity. This form of geotropism is exactly the reverse of that exhibited by roots. (See § 43.) Still another response to gravity is to be seen in the lateral branches of coniferous trees and trailing stems. These place their axes at right angles to the action of gravity. Sometimes the trailing habit is the result of the action of the plant in placing its axis at right angles to the rays of light which strike it. If the plant is placed in darkness, it may be found whether the horizontal position is

the result of the action of gravity or light. If it is the result of light, it will generally grow erect in darkness.

177. *Stems are found among the higher plants only.* — The seed plants and ferns only have true stems as determined by the tissues which compose them. The mosses, liverworts, and some of the seaweeds have a main axis from which branches are sent off, and while it performs the work of a stem it has not the true stem structures. A body of this kind is termed a *thallus.* The main axis of the mosses, liverworts, and the larger algæ is often designated as a stem, though it does not exhibit the distinction of tissues shown by the true stems of the higher plants.

K

VII. THE WAY IN WHICH NEW PLANTS ARISE

178. *Distribution of the individuals of a species.* —Every species is represented by a number of individuals. Sometimes this number is very great and may run up into the millions. On the other hand, there are a number of species of which but few individuals have been seen, and some are so rare that but a single specimen may have been found. The individuals of a species may be scattered across states and continents, or they may be congregated in a meadow or on a single mountain top. Thus, for instance, the common polypody forms carpets or dense layers on rocks, that contain several dozen of individuals, and these colonies may be found almost throughout North America, Asia, and Europe. The individuals of Adam-and-Eve, or putty root, occur one or a few in a place, in a broad belt of country that includes the northern half of the United States and the southern half of Canada. The Georgia oak (*Quercus Georgiana*)

is found only on the granite slopes of Stone Mountain in Georgia.

Every species originated in some one locality, and it spreads its seeds or spores by various methods. The spores or seeds find a foothold wherever they may in suitable places. Probably no species has succeeded in sending seeds or spores to all of the places which would be suitable for its growth. As the species spreads across a continent, it may meet barriers in the form of seas, mountains, or other obstacles which stop its progress.

179. *Methods of reproduction.* — The life of each individual is limited, and no matter whether the number is great or small, if each does not constantly give rise to new individuals the species would soon become exterminated. Furthermore new individuals must be produced as fast as the older ones die, or extermination will result. Numerous species of animals have disappeared in the memory of man, but modern examples of the extinction of plants are not common, although the earth's crust is rich with the remains of species existent in former geologic periods. A tree belonging to the sunflower family, once found on the island of Saint Helena, is known to be ex-

tinct. There are three principal methods by which new individuals may be formed: *vegetative reproduction* by means of *cuttings, buds, branches,* etc., simple or asexual *spores,* and *egg* formation.

180. *Reproduction by cuttings.*—Select a good healthy leaf of a begonia, cut it from the stem, trim away nearly half of it, and put the raw edge in sand kept moist in a shallow dish or box. Examine every week for a month. Roots will first be formed, and then if the experiment is allowed to run long enough a stem will appear, which will in turn bear leaves like the original from which the cutting was made. It is seen that the begonia is able to replace the entire plant from part of a leaf —a capacity that is shared by an extremely large number of species.

181. *The stem may reproduce the entire plant.*— Cut a small twig of the willow, a stem of the geranium, coleus, or begonia, and insert in moist sand as above. A few weeks later the cutting will be found to have replaced the missing roots and leaves and made a complete plant.

182 *The root may reproduce the plant.*—Cut off a portion of the fleshy root of a sweet potato or

horse radish, and put in moist sand or soil. Stems and leaves will be seen to appear after a time. The ability to replace the other members of the plant by the root is not very common. It is shared, however, by beech, cherry, poplar, and some coniferous trees.

183. *Structures used by plants as means of vegetative reproduction.* — Plants have many devices by which portions of the roots, stems, and leaves take on special forms and become separated from the parent plant in a manner which allows them to form a new individual. Chief among these structures are *bulbs* (see § 167), *bulbils*, *tubers*, *offsets*, *stolons*, besides many special forms.

184. *Tubers* — A tuber consists of a portion of an underground stem which serves as a storehouse for surplus food, and which is capable of reproducing the plant by the growth of its buds, which are usually several in number. Examine the base of a vigorous potato stem by digging away the soil. Besides the roots will be found numbers of thickened stems or potatoes. Note the "eyes," or buds, on the surface. Are they most abundant on the end toward the main stem or the apical end?

The main stem dies at the close of the season, leaving the tubers in the soil, and if each were capable of giving rise to one plant alone, the parent plant would be followed by a dozen or more the next season. This does not express the full reproductive power of the tubers, however. In the planting of " seed " potatoes to obtain a crop, the farmer cuts the tubers into pieces each of which contains an " eye " and is capable of giving rise to a new plant. As a consequence the tubers of a single plant may be capable of producing over a hundred new individuals.

Secure a large, sound potato in January and put it in the mouth of a large bottle filled with water, or a cup or tumbler, cover with a glass dish and set in a living room. Renew the water and clean the bottle occasionally. Note the manner in which the buds begin to grow and their location. Do all the buds awake? If several experiments have been set up, you can awaken the sleeping buds by destroying the active ones. Are new roots formed on the tuber or on the stems? Observe the behavior of potatoes which have sprouted in a dark cellar.

185. *Bulbils and bulblets.* — It has been shown how the underground branch enclosed in a bud

Missing Page

reddish cigar-shaped bulbils in the upper axils of the stems, which consist of a thickened branch sheathed by blunt scales. These structures drop from the plant in the autumn, and those which fall in the water, or those which are covered up by falling leaves, escape frost and germinate in the following spring, reproducing the plant. Those that drop into the water may be carried away by currents, and thus spread the species into unoccupied territory.

Cystopteris (*C. bulbifera*), a common fern, forms numerous bulblets on the lower surfaces of the midribs, which drop off in the autumn and germinate in the spring.

186. *Division of the body by the death of part of it.* — Some of the liverworts, club-mosses, ferns, and many of the seed plants have creeping underground stems which branch in the form of a letter Y. By the death of the older part of the stem, representing the base of the Y, the two branches are left as separate plants. These extend, branch, and divide in the same manner. Note this process in the common liverwort (*Marchantia*, or *Conocephalus*), in the *rhizomes* of the fern and club-moss. It may be seen also in the creeping grasses.

187. *Division among the simple plants.* — Among the forms in which the body consists of a single cell new ones are formed by the division of a parent cell, and the two halves quickly grow to the size of the original cell, when they divide in turn. Such organisms grow with great rapidity, and this method gives rise to a large number of individuals in a very short time. But fifteen or twenty minutes are necessary to enable each cell to attain full size and divide. By this method a single cell of a bacterium may produce sixteen million others in eight hours, and in a day many millions of millions.

188. *Runners.* — Many species of seed plants send out long branches with slender internodes from the bases of the main stalks, and these lie on the surface of the ground forming roots at each joint or node. Leaves are also formed, and later an upright stem. Then the runner itself dies away, leaving a young plant to mark the position of each node. This process may be followed in any strawberry bed, and is a very efficient method of spreading the plant.

189. *Stolons.* — The dewberries of pastures, some raspberries, and other plants, form slender stems

which finally lean over with their tips touching the ground. Roots are formed at this point, and the growth of leaves and a new main stem quickly follows, making a new individual.

190. *Dissemination or spreading of the plant by vegetative propagation.* — In all of the above methods by which new individuals are formed from portions of the body of a parent plant, the new specimen finds a foothold a greater or less distance from the parent. Each successive set of new plants is still farther away from the starting point, and it is to be seen that any species might travel considerable distances by such seemingly slow methods. Thus some of the young plants formed by the runners of a strawberry will be five feet from the parent, and as these quickly give rise to similar runners the species would travel across a large meadow in a few years.

191. *Gemmæ.* — If the upper surfaces of flat fronds of *Marchantia* or *Lunularia* are examined, small circular or crescent-shaped receptacles will be seen containing a number of globose masses of green tissue either loose or easily detached. These are the portions of its body devised to reproduce the species vegetatively, and are termed *gemmæ.* If

placed on damp soil covered with a dish in a warm room, they may be seen to germinate.

192. *Reproduction by spores.*—Instead of cutting off a member of its body for the purpose of giving rise to new individuals, the plant may develop special masses of reproductive tissue. When these masses reach maturity, they divide into a number of separate cells, each of which is capable of giving rise to a new individual upon germination. The origin of new individuals in this manner is termed *asexual reproduction*, and the spores in a puff ball, or those on the under side of a fern leaf, exhibit this action.

193. *Reproduction by eggs.*—In another method of reproduction the plant develops two kinds of reproductive tissue, and when these are mature a cell from each unite to form a fertilized egg, which then is capable of giving rise to a new individual. The two kinds of reproductive elements are termed *gametes*, and the origin of new plants by this method constitutes *sexual reproduction*.

194. *Fern spores.*—Examine the under side of the leaves or fronds of the polypody or any common fern in the autumn. A number of brown spots,

masses, or areas will be seen. After they are completely ripe, strike a sheet of white paper with the frond. A quantity of brownish particles will be thrown out on the paper. Examine with a lens. They appear to be roughened balls or egg-shaped masses. These are the asexual spores of the fern. Now examine the masses on the fern leaf with the lens. The spores have been enclosed in flasks or capsules with short stalks. Sometimes the collection of capsules is covered with a shield, or by the upturned edge of the frond.

Secure a small piece of a leaf of any common fern with mature spore cases. Allow it to become quite dry. Now lay it with the spore surface upward on a sheet of white blotting paper saturated with water, and cover with a glass dish. Remove the dish and examine a day later. Numerous brown spores will be seen scattered over the blotting paper in all directions. The spores are thrown out in a cloud by ferns in damp weather by the action of the capsules in which they are formed.

A great many of the mosses and liverworts are known also to reproduce themselves by means of various kinds of bulbils, cuttings, and similar parts, and this in many cases is the only way which they have of perpetuating the species.

195. *Germination of spores.* — Take a small piece of soft brick, and boil it thoroughly to kill all organisms attached to it. After it has been in the water for an hour, remove and set in a saucer of spring water. Cover with a tumbler. After it is cool sprinkle spores from some fern liberally over its surface. Replace the cover. Replenish the water in the saucer from time to time, keeping it in a comfortable living room in a dark corner. After a few weeks a number of greenish bodies will be seen on the brick. These have been produced by the germination of the spores.

196. *Another form or generation of the fern.* — The bodies produced by the germination of the spores are like small irregular leaves, and they are seen to adhere to the brick by means of hairs or rhizoids, which serve the purpose of fixing and absorbing organs. Now these flat bodies must be fern plants because they came from the spores of a fern. Their relation to the ordinarily known form may be ascertained if the culture is kept in order for a few weeks longer. Small upright stalks will appear,

bearing a minute leaf which gradually enlarges until it resembles that of the plant from which the spores were taken. A root may also be found. This young plant is attached to the leaflike body and apparently sprang from it. The young plant with a stem will enlarge, and if placed in the soil it would develop spores like those which were placed on the brick, and the life history of the species would be complete.

197. *Alternation of generations.* — In the complete life of the fern it is found to develop two individuals entirely different in form, and each gives rise to the other. This is known as the *alternation of generations.* One generation is constructed with a root, stem, and leaves, and it develops single spores which are capable of giving rise to the other generation. This large plant which is known to the ordinary observer is the *sporophyte.* The other generation is a *thallus,* or *prothallus,* and the body consists of a thin sheet of cells bearing green color, and furnished with rhizoids for absorption and fixation. This generation develops two kinds of reproductive cells in little flasks on the lower side of the prothallus. The flasks containing the *male gametes*

(§ 193) burst, and these elements find their way to the other flasks where the *female gametes* are developed, and one male gamete fuses with the female gamete, and the new cell thus formed gives rise to an individual of the other generation, which is the common fern plant. The prothallus form of the fern is then the *gametophyte.* In the fern the sporophytic generation is seen to be much the larger, and the higher one follows the development of the plant kingdom the greater will be the size of the sporophyte, and the smaller will be the gametophyte. On the other hand the gametophyte attains greater importance in some of the lower forms, as may be seen in the moss.

198. *The two generations of the moss.* — Secure a clump of a large moss, some of the specimens of which may be seen to be in "fruit." Examine one of the specimens which is not in "fruit." It will be found to consist of a small leafy stem, with perhaps rootlike organs arising from the lower end and furnished with rhizoids for absorption. The upper extremity of the stems bears leafy cups, in which are the organs containing the two kinds of gametes. This is the gametophyte of the moss. The male gametes

fuse with the female gametes, as in the fern, and the cell formed germinates without leaving its place as in the fern, but the structure of the individual formed is very much different. The second generation consists of a slender brownish or greenish stem, bearing a large capsule. This capsule is composed of tissue which contains chlorophyl, is furnished with a hood or other appendages, and contains a flask or sac, the contents of which develop into spores. The spores germinate and form the leafy stemmed plants examined at first, and the capsule and its stalk are thus the sporophyte of the moss. It is seen to be able to form some of its food by means of its chlorophyl, but it is dependent upon the gametophyte for its supply of water and mineral salts, and is sometimes said to be parasitic upon it.

199. *Occurrence of generations.* —This alternation of the two generations of a species is not invariable. It was found that by vegetative methods of reproduction (§ 180) the cutting reproduces its own generation in all the experiments tried. There are some instances, however, where the cutting of a sporophyte will produce a gametophyte, and *vice versa.* Then, again, the spores developed by the

sporophyte often grow into sporophytes upon germination. This is found in mushrooms and moulds. The mould which grows upon moist bread develops small sacs filled with spores, which take a black or brown color when ripe. These spores germinate and grow individuals exactly like those from which they sprung, without the formation of another generation. The asexual spores of the sporophyte may be observed if the umbrella-like top of a mushroom is carefully taken off and placed on a sheet of white paper for a day or two. The spores which are borne on the thin plates or *gills* on the under side of the *cap* are set free and fall upon the paper in great number. The germination of these generally produces a sporophyte.

200. *The generations of the seed plants.* — The species which produce flowers and seeds have two generations, but the gametophyte is so small that its behavior may not be seen without the use of special methods of observation with the compound microscope.

201. *The gametophyte, or egg-bearing generation in the seed plant.* — It was shown in the life history of the fern that unlike cells from different parts of

L

the body of the gametophyte were united to form
the fertilized egg from which a new plant was
formed, though this is not always the case.   In the
seed plants, however, the two kinds of gametes are
produced on different individuals, which are borne
on separate organs of the sporophyte, or on separate plants.   Thus the male gamete is produced in
a minute individual formed by the germination of
the pollen, and the female gamete in another imbedded deeply in the ovary.

202. *The structure of a flower.* — Secure a
fresh supply of flowers of the apple. This may
be done in winter by bringing in some twigs
of these trees, in the latter part of the winter,
and placing the lower ends in water for two or
three weeks before needed. The preparation should
be kept in a comfortable living room near a window. A supply of these or other suitable species
may be found out of doors during the proper season. When the fully opened blossoms have been
secured, note that the flower appears to sit in a
cup the upper edges of which divide into five leaflike bodies. The shape, size, and arrangement of
these will vary greatly in the several species

selected for observation. The separate parts of this cup, or circle, are usually termed *sepals,* and while they serve important uses in protecting other parts of the flower, or the fruit, yet they are not essential to reproduction, and are lacking in many species. Immediately inside the sepals is a circle of five large colored leaves, forming the most showy part of the flower; these are the *petals.* Like the sepals, they also exhibit great diversity in number, size, shape, and color in different species. Some are most beautifully painted and marked, and it is principally to the development of these organs in various plants that the florist's art is directed. These organs, also, play only a minor part in reproduction, and are lacking in many species.

Immediately inside the petals are to be seen a number of small knobs, or flasks, not much larger than a pin's head, borne on curved stalks. These are the *stamens,* and if the flasks are crushed or torn open, they will be found to contain a yellowish powder made up of a great number of *pollen grains.* In the centre of the flower are five small stalks extending up into the air, the *styles.* The expanded surface of the tip are the *stigmas.* The lower end of these styles terminates in a capsule buried in the tissues at the base of the flower. This capsule, if carefully cut across with a sharp knife, will be found to be divided into five chambers, correspondent to the number of styles, and it is termed the *ovary*, because it is in this organ that eggs are formed.   The ovary, styles, and stigma constitute the *pistil*.

Almost any flower will suffice for observations of the above character.   A dozen or more different kinds should be examined, noting the number, size, and arrangement of the different organs.   The greatest diversity will be found, indicating that the separate species accomplish the work of reproduction in a manner characteristic of themselves.

The flower described above is said to be *perfect*, but in others the stamens and pistils are in separate flowers on the same or different individuals.   The petals or the sepals may be absent or replaced by circles of bracts.   What is the arrangement of the organs in the jack-in-the-pulpit, spring beauty, buttercup, the ash tree, willow, beech, maple, and oaks? Examine also the flowers of the lily, trillium, larkspur, bean, and geranium.

203. *Spores of seed plants.* — The sporophytes of seed plants produce two kinds of spores. One is formed in the stamen and forms the pollen grains, and the other grows in the ovary and produces the gametophyte which bears the *egg* cells.

204. *Pollination.* — In order to complete the life history of the plant it is necessary that the pollen grains should be transported to the stigmas, or upper extremities of the pistils, where they may germinate and send a long tube down to the ovaries. Furthermore, it is important in a great number of species that the pollen from one plant should be carried to the pistils of another, a process termed by the botanist *cross pollination.* The seeds and seedlings obtained by this method are much stronger and represent the species more perfectly in most instances than those which result from the action of the pollen upon the pistil of the same flower. The various devices by which this cross pollination is secured are almost without number. One method by which the pollen of any flower is kept from its own pistil is to have the stamens and pistil mature at different times. In other cases the stamens are below the pistils, so that

the pollen would fall away from instead of upon
the pistil of the same flower.   Having guarded
against self-pollination, the plant must next be provided with means of securing pollen from other
flowers for all the pistils.   The principal agencies
which it makes use of in this work are the wind
and animals, principally insects.

205. *The wind as an aid to pollination.* — More
than ten thousand species are known to make use
of the wind as an agency in carrying the pollen from
one flower to another.   In order to do this success-
fully great quantities of pollen are produced and
thrown into the air upon the opening of the pollen
sacs, and then float upon the currents of air, some of
them alighting upon the stigmas of other flowers.
The pines, oaks, beeches, hazels, birches, poplars,
walnuts, mulberries, and some maples throw their
pollen into the air and allow it to float to other
flowers in this manner.   It is a matter of common
knowledge that when a single row of corn is planted
in a field with no other collection of the same in the
vicinity, generally no seeds are produced.   This will
always be the case if the row is at right angles to the
prevailing winds.   The pollen of the pines is often

thrown into the air in such quantities that it is deposited upon the ground, making a "shower of sulphur."

206. *Animals as pollen carriers.* — The flowers of many species are provided with means of attraction to certain animals, principally insects, and during their visits pollen adheres to their bodies and is carried to the next flower. The attraction may be nectar or honey, the pollen itself, a place for the deposit of eggs, or the flower may offer the insect a suitable place of refuge or lodgment for the night or during a storm. The description of the various methods by which this is done would fill a large book, and may not find place here. On a favorable day in the spring or summer the student should find a flower which is frequented by insects, and note the manner in which this visit is made. First determine the object of the visit. Then note what parts of its body rub against the stamens and pistils. Catch one of the insects, and examine its body for traces of pollen. Examine a number of flowers late in the evening or early in the morning for animals which have lodged in them during the night.

207. *Fertilization.* — When the pollen is carried
to the flower which it may benefit, it can only be of
use if it is deposited on or near the stigma at the top
of the pistil. Here it finds a sweetish and sticky
substance made up of cane sugar and glucose which
it uses as food in any growth it may make. If
properly placed on this stigma, the presence of this
sweetish substance starts it to germinating. A long
slender tube is produced, making a structure much
as if the head of a pin were to grow out and form
the body of the pin. The pollen tube is generally
very crooked and it bores into the sticky substance
in which the pollen grain is imbedded, and then
grows down into the style in an effort to get away
from the oxygen of the air. Not only does it strive
to get away from the oxygen of the air, but certain
substances in the ovary attract it. Now the tube
formed by the grain or pollen is a part of a gametophyte, and near its tip it contains a minute mass of
protoplasm, which is the male gamete which is to
be carried to the egg. The *embryo sac* in the
ovary contains the female gametophyte bearing an
egg cell, and the pollen tube extends to it, carrying the male gamete in its own tip. The union of
the gamete from each constitutes *fertilization*, and

the result is a structure from which a new sporophyte is formed. The ovary may be compound and contain many embryo sacs, in which case a separate pollen tube will be necessary to fertilize each one. The result will be many seeds or embryos separate or in a many-seeded fruit. The growth of the pollen tube down through the pistil to the embryo sac may take only a few hours, or it may occupy a year, as in the pines. Shortly after the fertilization of the egg it begins to grow and divide until an embryo plant of the sporophytic generation is formed, having possibly a root, a stem, and one, two, or more seed leaves with the main growing point of the future stem.

VIII. SEEDS AND FRUITS

208. *The seed.* — After the embryo has reached a certain stage of development it becomes quiescent and remains so until the time and opportunity arrives for it to grow in the germination of the seed. During the development of the embryo from the egg, reserve foods for its use during germination in the shape of *oil, starch, sugar,* or *protein* may be deposited in its seed-leaves, or in the seed-coats, or in other organs developed for that purpose.

209. *The existence of the seed.* — Generally about the time that the embryo has completed growth and the deposit of food has been made, the seed or fruit is separated from the parent plant, though this is not always the case. Germination of the seed takes place when it secures proper conditions of *season, moisture,* and *temperature.* This may be in a few days or several years. Some seeds actually grow before separation from the parent plant, while others may remain quiescent during the lifetime of a man.

Stories are current of seeds being taken from mummy cases six thousand years old which showed powers of germination, but such statements are not authentic. Instances are known in which certain species have lived three hundred or even four hundred years, but these probably represent the limit attainable by only a few plants. Ordinary forms, such as wheat and corn, may not live longer than fifteen or twenty years at the utmost, and the seeds of nearly all cultivated plants begin to show lessening powers of germination after a year. Some are totally worthless the second year.

210. *Fruits.* — In addition to the coats formed around the seed the portions of the ovary in contact with the seed are often developed in certain ways of benefit or assistance in the protection, dissemination, or germination of the seeds. The seed and all of the parts of the ovary adhering to it constitute a *fruit*. The study of the structure and behavior of the fruit after the ripening of the seed will therefore be of great interest.

211. *The cocoanut.* — The fruit of *Cocos nucifera* offers a most interesting object for the illustration of the action and structure of the fruit of

a palm. The material necessary for the work consists of a few stripped nuts, such as are offered for sale in every village, and some from which the husks have not been taken. The latter may be obtained from merchants dealing extensively in tropical fruits.

Two or more each of the whole fruits, and the same number of stripped nuts, should be placed in moist sawdust or soil in a box two or three times its size, and kept in a comfortable living room or greenhouse if the work is to be done in winter. In the summer it may be placed in the ground like any seed. The time necessary for germination is from six to ten weeks. This will furnish germinated seeds for examination, and will also show whether the husk is necessary for germination or not.

I. *Size and appearance of the fruit.*

   Make an examination of the entire fruit, and note : —

   a. The shape of the base and apex, and general form of fruit. Three wide short *bracts* may be found adhering to the base; these are from the envelopes of the flower, and may be the *calyx*. The blunt angles may be seen to run from the base to the apex. Draw.

b. Measure the circumference, length, and diameter. Place in a bucket of water. Does it float? Will the stripped nut float? Plunge the fruit into a bucket exactly filled with water. Remove and refill the bucket. The amount of water necessary to refill the bucket will be the volume of the fruit. Many of the fruits drop from the trees into the water of streams, ponds, and tides, and are carried long distances before they lodge and germinate. The planters place the fruits in the margins of salt lagoons and marshes, and the salt is supposed to hasten the process of germination.

II. *Structure.*

Cut through a fruit crosswise by means of a sharp saw, and note : —

a. *The husk*, the outer layer of which is smooth and firm, while the mass is composed of strong *fibres* and *pith*. Observe the attachment of the husk to the *shell*.

b. Strip the husk from the entire fruit, and note its relative thickness over different parts of the shell. Note also the character of the fibres at the basal end. The husk is derived from the wall of the ovary. If the fruit were suspended on its stem and were broken off suddenly, which end would strike the ground first? Do you think this beneficial or not?

Examine the stripped nut and note:—

c. The shape and markings of the shell. The three dark circular areas on the basal end are the marks of the three parts or *carpels* of the *ovary*.

Break or cut up the nut and test —

d. The hardness of the shell. Cut with knife and test strength. Is it " air tight " and " water tight " ?

The husk is derived from the outer wall of the ovary, and the shell from the inner wall, neither being seed-coats.

III. *The seed.*

Examine the nut which has been cut, and note: —

a. The central cavity, filled with a sweetish

clear fluid, the " milk." Determine the capacity of this central cavity.

b. The white layer of " meat," the *endosperm,* which is composed of storage cells containing reserve food. Apply a drop of iodine as a test for the presence of starch. The endosperm plainly contains oil, for it is expressed in great quantities in factories. Sugar may be detected by the taste. Split off portions of the endosperm and measure its thickness.

c. A brownish membrane will be seen adhering to the outer surface of the endosperm, which is made up of the true *seed-coats.*

IV. *The embryo.*

Working from the inside, carefully cut away the endosperm from around the eyes.

a. Under one of them will be found an irregular white cylinder, about a third of an inch long, with the outer flattened end pressed against the seed-coat, and the inner portion buried in the endosperm.

This is the young plantlet. There was originally an egg apparatus under each eye, but two of them have not been given an opportunity for development, and the whole ovary is devoted to the nourishment and protection of one embryo. Rarely two embryos are perfected in one fruit, making twin trees when they germinate. Make a drawing of the embryo.

V. *Germination.*

Carefully cut away one side of the germinated fruit, being careful not to injure the young plant, and note: —

a. *The absorbing organ,* the inner end of the embryo, which is made of the *cotyledon,* has developed a mass of tissue, very much the shape of a puff-ball, which is at first the size of a marble, but which gradually enlarges until it fills the cavity of the nut. It uses the milk for food as it grows, and furthermore it secretes digestive fluids (*enzyms*), which dissolve the starch and oil in the endosperm, about as it would be done in the human stomach. The fluid thus obtained is conveyed back into the young plant and serves as food. The endosperm may be seen to be thinner where the absorbing organ has touched it. The amount of food furnished by the endosperm is so great that the plantlet may be nourished many months from it alone, and generally it is entirely consumed, remaining sweet and sound as long as a trace is present.

b. The outer end of the cylindrical part of the embryo contains the *plumule,* or young shoot of the plant, and the root, which pushes through the eye, breaking the thin layer of the shell at that point, when the plumule, a conical mass of firm leaves, bores upward through the fibres of the husk. When light is reached, green leaves are formed.

The main root goes downward, sending out branches which break through the husk at various points, finally penetrating the soil. If the fruits have been

M

germinated in the spring, the plantlets may endure the summer out of doors in almost any part of the United States.

The cocoanut has its original habitat in the Eastern hemisphere, but now occupies the tropics around the globe. This wide distribution has been secured by the agency of wind and water, and by the attractive power of the food, stored up in the endosperm, for tribes of savage and civilized men.

212. *The date.* — The fruit of the commercial date may be easily obtained, and used to illustrate the action of the fruit of a second palm.

Secure a few dozen dried dates, such as are sold by grocers and confectioners, and place a dozen in the soil in a pot kept at a temperature about equal to that of a comfortable living room, three or four weeks before the observations are to be begun. Strip the fleshy part of the fruit of a second dozen and put in a second pot and place with the first. This will show whether the edible flesh is of any benefit in the actual process of germination. Soak another lot in water for two weeks for dissection.

I. *The appearance of the fruit.*

Place some of the fruits in water for an hour, and then note : —

    a. The general appearance, size, and form.

    b. The outer covering; is it a distinct membrane, or a part of the flesh underneath, as in the husk of the cocoanut?

    c. The edible, fleshy portion; is it attached to the seed?

II. *The seed.*

    a. Describe the form of the seed.

    b. Test the hardness and brittleness of the seed and its coats. Crush or break the seed to determine its firmness.

    c. Cut away the coats from the surface of the seed opposite the groove, and note the position of the tip of the main root of the embryo.

    d. Cut the seed across and take out the embryo. Describe its form and draw.

III. *Germination.*

Cut across some of the germinating seeds in the same manner, and note: —

    a. Absorbing organ, the cotyledon, here as

in the cocoanut, serves as a digesting
and absorbing organ. It develops as
a cylindrical mass, and its juices corrode
the hard *cellulose* of the seed which is
stored as food for the young plantlet.
The absorbing organ expands until it
consumes all of the cellulose, and finally
fills up the entire space inside the coats.

b. Sketch the development of the basal end
of the cotyledon. It elongates and
forces the embryo stem tipped with the
root downward through the soil. As it
does so it opens at one side and allows
the first green leaf of the plumule to
come out. Finally the root begins to
develop, and it continues the downward
course taken by the cotyledon. If the
seeds were in the dry soil in which
the plant grows, the root and cotyledon
would bore down more than a yard before any branches would be given off.
But in the pot cultures this is impossible and unnecessary, for the plant finds
sufficient moisture near at hand. So far
as can be found from an examination of

the date seed, without seeing the plant in its native habitat, the only manner in which this fruit would secure the dissemination of the seed would be by means of its pleasant tasting fruit, which would cause it to be sought for food by animals in general, some of which, including man, in using it would carry the fruit some distance from the parent tree. This use of the fleshy portion for food does not in any way affect the germinating power of the seed, so long as it is not cooked. Furthermore, the seeds are capable of enduring great extremes of heat and cold, and may lie around on the surface of the soil for months or even years, and then grow when the proper conditions for germination are given them.

213. *Maize, or Indian corn.* — Maize, or the ordinary Indian corn, is a third example of the plants belonging to the same general group as the palms, and it is even more interesting than the fruits just examined. In order to see clearly the pur-

poses and nature of these fruits, one should have some entire ears which have been brought in with the husk and are still attached to the stalk, or, at least, a section of it.

I. *The arrangement and protection of the fruits.*

Examine the external characters of the ear and its covering, and note : —

a. *The silks*, hanging in a reddish-brown tuft from the tip.

b. The texture of the *husks*, and the manner in which they cover the ear. Remove one at a time, and compare the outer and inner husks.

c. Take one of the " silks," and follow it to its inner end. To what is it attached ?

d. The great number of fruits arranged in parallel rows on the central stalk or " cob." Estimate the number of the grains.

e. The attachment of the grain to the cob. The scales.

f. *The cob.* Cut or break it across, and describe its structure.

II. *The grains or seeds.*

Place a number of seeds in moist earth ten days
before the observations are to be made, and
a few in water a day beforehand. Examine
the soaked seeds, and note : —

a. The forms, size and outward appearance.
Compare the two broader sides.

b. Remove the outer membrane which covers
the seed. This is composed not only of
the two seed-coats, but also of layers
from the walls of the ovary, which it
would be impossible to separate without
the use of methods which need the compound microscope.

c. The seed is composed of two parts : the
embryo, which occupies the space under
the whitish area on one side, and the
mass of endosperm, or stored food.

d. Examine the endosperm, and test with a
drop of iodine. It is this portion of the
grain that is chiefly used for food by man

III. *The embryo.*

Remove the entire embryo from a softened
grain, and note : —

a. Its general shape. Sketch.

b. The scutellum, or absorbing organ, the part which lies under the embryo and in contact with the endosperm. If germinated seeds are examined, this organ will be seen to have enlarged and taken up some of the endosperm, as in the date or cocoanut. It has the power of secreting digestive fluids, which dissolve starch and convert it into sugar. The action of this fluid on the endosperm soon causes it to become soft, and then milky fluid.

c. The young plantlet shows an unrolling leaflet, a short stem, and a main root. Describe the action of these organs in germination. Note the formation of young roots above the base of the main roots. These are the stilt roots, which are so prominent on the full-grown plant (§ 29).

IV. *Endurance of the seeds.*

Put a number of sound grains into a covered vessel full of water, set on the stove, and allow the water to boil. Place an equal number of grains on the cover of the vessel, but where they will be dry. Plant both lots of seeds in the soil, and note: —

a. The number that germinate. What do you conclude as to the power of the grain to resist extremes of heat?

Put a number of grains in a shallow dish of water in the morning, and set outside where they may freeze at night. Place alongside these an equal number in a dry dish. Now put both lots in separate boxes of moist soil, keep in a comfortable living room, and note: —

b. The number germinating. What do you conclude as to the power of the grains to resist cold?

The capacity of the seed to endure heat or cold is very great. The seed of a plant is capable of undergoing much greater extremes of climate than the adult plant, which is largely due to the fact that it contains very little water. Thus a seed if kept dry may be exposed to a heat which will boil water and still germinate, but if actually put into boiling water and permitted to absorb the warm liquid, it will be killed. On the other hand, seeds of many common plants may be bathed in liquid hydrogen at a temperature of four hundred and twenty degrees below freezing point and still retain the power of germination.

V. *The dissemination of the seeds.*

    a. Could dissemination take place by water or wind ?

    b. If you can observe a field of corn, note whether any animals carry away the grains or not, and if so what is done with them. Are all of them destroyed ? It would also be interesting to make similar observations on the acorns of the oaks.

    Man has been an important factor in the distribution of corn, and his method of growing and treating it has resulted in the development of new species and varieties. It is cultivated over great areas, and although the larger number of the seeds produced annually are used as food, yet enough are preserved to perpetuate the species, so that this plant is represented by many millions of individuals in regions where it would have none if it were not for man. Thus without the interference of man corn could not grow and seed from year to year in any place in northern United States.

214. *The fruit of the clot-bur, Xanthium.* — The fruits of this plant, which is a relative of the sunflower, are very much different from those previously examined, both in structure and action. The plant is a weed, and it is more or less abundant over a great part of the United States. The fruits may be taken from the plant in August or September, picked up from the ground or taken from the coats of animals in late autumn.

I. *External appearance of fruit.*

Examine the clusters of four or five fruits, and note their position on the plant as well as the following features : —

a. The prongs at the apex, and the hooked

bristles over the remainder of the fruit. Make a drawing, showing form and arrangement of bristles.

  b. Cut across the fruit, and note the structure of the outer walls which bear the bristles, and that the fruit is *two-seeded*.

II. *The seeds.*

  a. The seeds are unequal in size.

  b. The seed-coats are distinct in texture and color. Describe.

III. *The embryo.*

  a. The embryo seems to fill the entire seed. The food is stored up in two oblong oval leaflike bodies, the *cotyledons,* which are whitish in color.

  b. The *plumule,* or young leaves, may be found between the cotyledons and the short main root below them. Draw the embryo.

IV. *Germination.*

  a. Examine twenty seeds which have lain in moist soil for a month, and from each fruit generally but one plantlet will have grown. Take up the fruit which is still attached to the single germinated embryo. The other seed has not shown any signs of growth.

b. Take a number of these fruits from which one plantlet has sprung, and put them in a pot and set out of doors for a season. Many of them will be found to germinate the second seed.

c. Examine the young plant, and note the position and growth of the cotyledons. What becomes of them? How does the root develop? The single cotyledon of the species previously examined did not come out of the seed-coats; what is the behavior in this instance?

d. Strip the seeds of several fruits, being careful not to injure them, and find whether they will germinate alone.

215. *Nature of fruits of Xanthium.* — The fruits of Xanthium are seen to be adapted for the dissemination of the seeds by becoming fastened or entangled in the coats of animals, and thus are carried long distances from the parent plant. In the case of migratory animals this method might

carry them the length or breadth of a continent, across wide seas, or over mountain ranges.

The Xanthium has an additional device not found on any other known plant. This is the manner in which the *paired* seeds germinate, one the first year and the other the second. This method would enable it to gain a foothold in places where it otherwise might not. Thus, when the fruit is carried to a field or dropped along the path of the animal to which it has been attached, the coming of the spring season sets one seed in action and a plant-let is produced. This may survive and produce a crop of fruits, in which case the species will easily hold its own in this locality. On the other hand, the young plant may be trampled to death by the same animal which brought it to the place, it may be overshadowed by other species which grow more luxuriantly, or the watchful farmer may take this opportunity to destroy one of the worst enemies of his crops. The destruction of the first seedling from any cause, however, still leaves the species another chance to gain a foothold in this locality, for at the beginning of the second season the other seed germinates and begins the struggle for exist-ence for the species all over again.

The fruit of the Xanthium then is not only furnished with a device for securing transportation from any animal that touches its fruits, but after the fruits have reached a spot favorable for growth, only half the seeds are germinated, the remainder ·being held in reserve for a second attempt which may be more successful than the first. Thus, if at this moment every plant of this species were destroyed, there would still remain the second seeds of the fruits which have sent up but one plantlet and kept the other in the form of a seed.

216. *The apple.* — The fruit of the apple offers a most interesting study, not only on account of the structure, but also because of the manner in which it has succeeded in attracting the attention of animals, particularly man, and has thus secured dissemination over an immense area of the earth's surface. During this process it has also undergone great changes as a result of the methods of cultivation by which it has been grown.

In the examination of the flower of the apple it was seen that the ovary was imbedded in a small greenish capsule, and that the parts of the flower appeared to stand on top of it (§ 202). All of the parts of a flower really spring from the end of the flower-stalk, so that this young apple consists of the bases of the petals, sepals, stamens, and pistils fused together. The fruit of the apple is thus composed of portions derived from all of the organs of the flower. Cut across a mature apple in the middle, and note in the exact centre : —

a. *The core.* — It is seen to be joined directly to the stem at the base of the apple, and terminates at the other end in some small dried appendages, which cannot be made out in a ripe apple. If a half-grown specimen is secured fresh from a tree, it will be seen that the five styles of the pistil are attached to the core. Down in the centre of the core will be found five small chambers containing seeds ; the pistil of this plant was therefore compound, and each of the five styles furnished a passageway for pollen tubes to the egg-cells in the chambers at its base.

Make out the *membrane* lining the seed cavities, or cells. Examine the *flesh* of the apple. Note the outer *skin*. It is often very strong and is covered with a layer of wax. What is the difference between the flesh of apples which may be kept for a long time, and those which rot shortly after they ripen ?

The membrane which lines the cavity of the cells containing the seed corresponds to the pod of a pea in being the wall of the ovary, and the flesh is derived from the calyx and perhaps a part of the stalk. The calyx and stamens are seen adhering to the flesh in half-grown fruits.

Examine the seed with respect to its coats and methods of germination.

The fruit of the apple attracts animals by the food which it offers them, and in the use of this fruit the seeds would be carried some distance from the parent tree. This method operated both with regard to man and lower animals in earlier times. Later, since man has developed the art of improving or increasing its fruit-bearing capacity in order to derive still more benefit from it, the apple has had a very peculiar history. The edibility of its fruit has still been the attractive feature, and this has secured the wide dissemination of the apple, not by the seeds which the fruit contains, but it has induced man to propagate it by means of cuttings. The cuttings are sometimes grown directly in the soil, as in other forms discussed in a previous paragraph. By a method of grafting, or causing a shoot of one tree to adhere and grow to the body of

N

another, special varieties are propagated without the use of seed. The forms developed in this method are very widely different from the type of the species, and when a seed of a fruit borne on one of these grafted branches is planted, it produces a tree which is unlike the characteristic branch from which it sprung, and it is said not to " come true." As a matter of fact the seedling does come true to the species, but not to the cutting or grafted branch from which it sprung.

217. *The bean and pea.* — Examine a flower of the bean and pea. Note the characters of the different parts of the flower. Describe the number and arrangement of the stamens and pistils. Is pollination aided by the wind or animals? Follow the development of the pistil. From what is the pod derived? Note the manner in which the pods open, and the position of the seeds which fall upon the ground. How far are they thrown from the parent plant? Do the pods open forcibly?

Describe and draw the outward appearance and form of the seeds. Note the number and character of the coats.

A number of peas and beans should be placed in

the soil two weeks before the observations are to be made, and a similar number in a tumbler with damp blotting paper three or four days before. Dissect one of each kind which has been treated in the latter way. The seed is made up almost entirely from two large swollen seed leaves or cotyledons, which readily separate when the coats are removed. At one side, holding the cotyledons together, may be seen the young plant, consisting of the *root, embryonic stem*, and the *minute leaves*, or plumule. To what part are the cotyledons attached?

If the seeds which were placed in the soil in boxes or in the ground are now observed, the behavior of the cotyledons may be followed. Both contain the reserve food for the young plant, and yield it as needed. What position do the cotyledons take in each case? How long do they endure, and what is their fate? Make drawings illustrating the points made.

The development of the leaves also offers a point of interest. Make drawings of the first, second, and third leaves of the bean, and note the difference in their structure. Make drawings and note form of the five leaves which appear first on the stem of the pea. It will be seen in both instances that the first leaf that appears is simple, the blade not being divided or branched. In the bean it is an active green leaf, but in the pea it is a small three-pointed scale or bract which is not very conspicuous and may be easily overlooked. The second leaf will show greatest difference from the first in the bean, and the third of that plant will be very nearly the form seen on the adult stems. The second leaf of the pea, however, is but little more developed than the first, but the third, fourth, and fifth show increased development. Perhaps not until the sixth or seventh leaf is reached will you find the characteristic leaf of the pea. The incomplete or simple leaves of seedlings are termed embryonic leaves, and it is a theory of the botanist that they represent forms used by the species in earlier stages of its history, and these leaves are the leaves of its ancestors, slightly changed of course. Thus many thousands or millions of years ago the group of plants from which beans have sprung were furnished with simple leaves like those shown just above the cotyledon. Later these plants began to form lobes in the lamina, and finally it was branched or divided as in the modern bean. There may be still other stages between these, or before any of them, which are lost. For while the plant may repeat a part of its ancient history, we cannot be quite sure that it has recounted all of it. In fact, it would be almost impossible for it to do so. In the instance of the pea, the bracts or first leaves may be simply the bases of incomplete organs and may not represent the lamina at all.

IX. THE POWER OR ENERGY OF THE PLANT

218. *Energy in the plant.* — In the preceding paragraphs the plant has been shown to do a great many kinds of work, and to use great force or power in carrying out these processes. The pushing of roots through the soil, the movements of these and other organs, the lifting of the food from the soil to the top of the stems, the pumping of the water from the roots to the leaves, — a distance which may be as great as five hundred feet, — are examples of external forms of work done by the plant. The living plant is only a machine, and it cannot originate or give rise to energy any more than a steam engine may. The engine is simply a device for using the energy released when fuel is burned in its furnaces. This energy in the form of heat converts water into steam, and it may be conducted through pipes and made to act in a manner convenient to the operator.

219. *Sources of energy.* — The plant receives energy from sunlight, and from the chemical com-

pounds which it absorbs from the soil, and also makes use of the physical energy exhibited by certain substances.

220. *Sunlight as a source of energy.* — The portion of sunlight absorbed by leaves is used as a means of separating compounds in such manner that the parts of these compounds will form new and more powerful unions. It is as if one had two magnets, to each of which was adhering a small bar of iron. By the use of a small amount of force the magnets and the iron may be separated, and then the magnets will mutually attract each other with greater force. Sunlight tears away some of the oxygen united with the magnet hydrogen to form water, and some of the oxygen united with the magnet carbon in carbon dioxide, leaving the carbon and hydrogen to rush together, forming a stronger chemical union and carrying with them a portion of the oxygen.

221. *Chemical compounds as a source of energy.* — Animals get all their energy from chemical compounds used as food. The foods of the plant are very simple compounds, but they gain some energy in this manner.

222. *Physical attraction as a source of energy.* — Compounds often exert an attraction for each other, and the resulting union does not change the composition of either of them. Thus sugar and salt attract water, and will even draw it from the air; but when sugar and water come together, they form a solution, and the composition of neither is disturbed. The water may be driven off and the sugar will remain as before. Examples of this were seen in the experiments illustrating the action of the root-hair.

223. *Release of energy.* — After energy has been acquired by the plant, it may be transformed or released and made to do various kinds of work. The principal method of releasing energy is the same as that used in the steam engine, and consists in *oxidizing* or *burning* the compounds which contain it.

224. *Respiration or breathing.* — The slow burning of material goes on almost constantly in all living substance, and it is essentially the same kind of a process in both plants and animals. It is most rapid in growing tissues and slowest in resting seeds and spores. It is still maintained, however, and it

is this slow burning up of the protoplasm which is responsible for the death of old seeds. At extremely low temperatures it ceases, as do all the activities of protoplasm. Thus when seeds are placed in liquid air at a temperature of nearly three hundred degrees below zero, Fahrenheit, it can be stated with certainty that breathing as well as all other activities have ceased.

225. *Changes in the air produced by breathing.* — The oxygen used in breathing is sometimes taken from compounds in the plant, and then the burning is sometimes incomplete, and no external evidence of it can be seen. In one form, however, marked changes are made in the air. This may be detected by the following experiment. Secure three fruit jars and fill one half-full of peas which have been soaked in water for a day, put the same quantity of dried peas in the second, and allow the third to remain empty. Cover tightly. A day later prepare a small torch by fastening a section of a candle an inch long to a piece of wire a foot long. A bit of string soaked in oil will answer equally well. Light the torch, remove the cover of the empty jar, and lower the blaze into it. The flame

remains unchanged. Repeat with the jar of dried seeds. No effect is noticeable. Repeat with the germinating seeds. The blaze is extinguished. Relight and test again. The extinguishment of the blaze has a double meaning. The oxygen of the air, which is necessary to support the blaze, has been used by the germinating seeds for their burning. In its place is the carbon dioxide which has been produced, which now forms one-fifth of the air in the jar.

The burning of the quiescent dry seeds is so slow that it has not produced any change in the air about them. The second and third jars show that it is not the influence of the jar which extinguishes the blaze.

The above experiment may be performed with mushrooms, flowers, or any portion of the living plant which does not contain chlorophyl. Breathing is carried on by all parts of the plant, but the portions which contain chlorophyl take up the carbon dioxide thirty times faster than it is formed by the same organ. Thus, if green plants were enclosed in the jar the carbon dioxide would be quickly used, and the amount of oxygen increased.

226. *Plants by day and by night.* — During the daytime the green plant takes up thirty times as

much carbon dioxide as it gives off, and throws off thirty times as much oxygen as it uses   At night, however, it burns and exhibits only the action of the germinating seeds. This has led to a popular belief that living plants in a sleeping room have an unhealthful effect on the occupant because of the carbon dioxide which they throw off. Such effects are largely imaginary, because all the plants which could be crowded into a bedroom would not give off as much carbon dioxide as a single candle.

227. *Relation of the living world and the atmosphere.* — It is also a common impression that the activities of plants and animals balance each other in maintaining the composition of the atmosphere, and it will be profitable to recall some of the general facts bearing upon this question.

A single person throws about two pounds of carbon dioxide into the atmosphere daily, and the total product of the human race for twenty-four hours is twenty-seven or twenty-eight hundred million pounds. The breathing of the lower animals and plants and the products of fires bring the total amount of carbon dioxide produced daily by living beings directly and indirectly to about six thousand

million pounds. Fifty square yards of leaf surface
will take up as much carbon dioxide as may be
thrown off by a single person, and furnish as much
oxygen as he would need. When the immense area
of the leaves of all the plants in the world is considered, it is found at the extremest low estimate
that the vegetable world uses more than twice as
much carbon dioxide as may be produced by living
agencies, and gives off twice as much oxygen as
they consume. No appreciable change has ever
been found in the composition of the atmosphere
with respect to these gases, however, and it must
be concluded that other agencies are at work which
use these gases; otherwise the air would be growing poorer in carbon dioxide and richer in oxygen.

It is found that changes are constantly going on
in the soil and in the rocks, which liberate and
take up these gases in quantities which make the
amounts used by living things seem very insignificant,
and that the waters of the sea form a vast storehouse for them. Then again the atmosphere contains about eight thousand billions of pounds of
carbon dioxide, and if the activities of plants were
to cease entirely, it would be many hundreds of
years before the proportion of gases would be

altered sufficiently to be sensible to any other living thing.

Furthermore, plants are capable of using nearly two hundred times as much carbon dioxide as they now get in the atmosphere, so that there is no actual balance between plants and animals so far as the atmosphere is concerned.

228. *Energy of physical attraction.* — It has been seen that the attraction of sugar for water results in pulling water into the plant containing food. It is also known that this same action carries fluids from one part of the body to another, and serves especially in aiding to carry the current of water from the roots to the leaves. It is this power of attraction of one substance for another which fills the cells with water, making them tense and firm. The firmness of the cells filled with water in this manner is all that holds up the soft stems of herbaceous plants When the water is driven off by heat this work is no longer accomplished, and the stems wilt and fall over. Water is attracted into the cells by certain substances, and if substances with stronger attractive power are placed outside the plant, the water will be with-

drawn from the cells, and the plant will become as limp as if it were wilted in the sun. Cut off the plump, rapidly growing shoots of any soft-bodied plant and lay them in a deep dish which contains water saturated with sugar or salt. Examine after a few hours. The shoots will be found limp and weak, and bend over when you attempt to hold them upright by the basal parts of the stems.

229. *Outward work accomplished by physical attraction.* — When water is attracted into a cell the cell expands with a force which may be equal to twenty times the pressure of the atmosphere. The expansion of the cells of a root will split apart rocks and perform similar work. This may be demonstrated as follows: Fill a narrow-necked bottle of a capacity of four to eight ounces with dried peas. Next pour in as much water as the bottle will hold, and then, without admitting air, invert the bottle, and set the mouth in a dish of water. Examine a day or two later. The cells of the seeds will have taken in so much water under the attractive power of the substances which they contain that they have expanded and burst the walls of the bottle.

X. RELATIONS OF PLANTS TO EACH OTHER AND THEIR HABITAT

230. *Societies and communities.* — All living things exist in the form of *societies* and *communities*, in a manner which is fairly well illustrated by the mode of life of the human family. Men attempt to live in the places where they may most easily obtain food, clothing, and shelter, and enjoy comfort. Nearly every man devotes his energy to certain kinds of work, and lives in a suitable house so far as possible for him to do so. It may be readily seen that the men devoted to one trade could not form a community. Thus the tailors, tinners, blacksmiths, carpenters, and merchants could not separately form communities, for a community is made up of representatives of each of these and many other kinds of workers. A community comprises the people in a town, village, city, or a region of the country occupied by a village and outlying land, according to the habits of the people. Generally some one trade or group of workers occupies the most prominent place in the community, and this causes it to be

spoken of as a farming community, a mining camp or town, a manufacturing town or city, a fishing village or shipping town, according to the kind of work most prominent in its affairs.

231. *Plant societies.* — The plants of different areas on the earth's surface are unlike in general form, are made up of different species, and secure the things essential to life in very different manners, and constitute a community. The principal communities in northern United States are *forests, meadows, swamp societies, pond societies, beach marshes, thickets, heaths, moors, sand,* and *rock societies,* beside many others of more or less frequent occurrence. The general aspect of a society in the landscape is determined by its largest or most prominent member. Thus, for instance, if the chief member is a tree, the community will be a forest. Further, the forest goes by the name of the most abundant tree, and there are oak forests, beech, maple, and pine forests or communities. In many cases communities have taken on the names of the place in which they live, as in swamp, rock, beach, and sand societies.

232. *Foundations of society.* — The things which determine the character of any plant community

are, — *the water supply, temperature of the soil and air, physical and chemical properties of the soil, winds, and light.* The length of time during which these conditions have continued unchanged in any given piece of land or country is also a very important factor.

233. *Communities change.* — Communities are always in a state of being changed, and they may disappear from any place and others may replace them. A good example of this will be seen if a marsh or pond is drained. During the existence of the pond, water societies only could live there. The mud left by the pond will allow societies of lower plants to form a green coating over its surface. After a time liverworts, mosses, and ferns may find suitable conditions here. Later, when the mud has dried and the soil becomes loose and loamy, flowering plants will find a foothold, and if undisturbed, young trees may grow up, and thus the place once occupied by a pond society will be the residence of a forest. But even then the changes are not all past. The action of the first kind of trees on the soil may fit it for the growth of other trees, and the first forest may be replaced by a different one. Similar move-

o

ments have been followed in the development of human societies. The hunter and the pioneer first occupy the soil or land, to be followed by the miner and the farmer, and then by the manufacturing town or the city.

234. *Water and plants.* — The plant is extremely sensitive about its supply of water. Not only must it have a certain amount of rainfall each year, but the rain must be given throughout the whole year, instead of all at one time. The amount capable of being retained by the soil and the salts it contains are also of importance. The pond societies float in or on top of the water, or are submerged beneath it.

235. *Temperature and plants.* — Each species requires a certain number of warm days for its development and can endure only certain low temperatures. Thus our summers in the Middle states are warm enough for the castor-oil plant out of doors, but the low temperatures of winter kill it. The warmth-retaining value of the soil is to be taken into account in this connection. The surface of the country is also a feature. In broken hilly regions the cold air settles down in the valleys, making

them much colder than the near-by hill-tops, and these valleys are much warmer in the daytime than the hills.

236. *The soil and plants.* — The chemical character of the soil with respect to the kind and amount of food it contains, and its physical qualities due to its coarseness or fineness, and power to hold water, as well as its heating properties, influence the communities growing upon it. The principal soils are *rock, sand, lime, humus* or *loam*, and *clay*. Beside the soil itself, the coverings of *snow, leaves*, or *living plants* are of value to the community.

237. *Light and plants.* — Light is necessary for all green plants, but some are able to make use of rays of less intensity than others, and have altered the structure of their entire bodies to suit this adaptation. The species which can use the weaker light usually stand under those that require the full blaze of the sun, in the shadow of rocks, on northern slopes, or if they are aquatic species they live at some depth under the surface of the water. Along a sea beach the area between high and low water which is thus exposed to the full force of the sun part of every day is inhabited by green, brown, and

red seaweeds. The top layer of water extending to a depth of a hundred and fifty feet is inhabited by red and some brown algæ, and below this depth for a short distance the red algæ alone find suitable conditions. Bacteria may live at depths of over half a mile or in complete darkness, in the same manner that mushrooms or other non-green species may live in caves completely shut off from the light.

238. *Wind and plants.* — The wind affects the character of the stems developed, and is a very important factor in carrying pollen from one flower to another, disseminating seeds, spores, and other reproductive bodies. Its general direction is an important factor in determining the rainfall also.

239. *Forests.* — The best idea of a community may be gained from the study of one as it lives in an undisturbed condition, and it will be most profitable to make the first observations on the subject in a forest, since the relations of its members are more easily determined than in some others.

In order that the work upon this point should have any great value it should be extended throughout the greater part of a season, though many features of interest may be made out in a single visit.

It will be found most convenient to select the most accessible forest and make visits of several hours each to it on several days, which may be a week or a month apart. This may be done by using the weekly holiday for excursions, which may also be made the opportunity of collecting material for other experiments, and for the observation of reproduction, dissemination of seeds and fruits, action of leaves, etc. It is indispensable that some member of the party should be able to identify the common species of plants found in the community, and it will be highly profitable and necessary that all should use a manual in taking the census of the flora.

On the first visit to the forest walk over its entire area, or enough of it to gain a general idea of its extent, the character of its surface, whether level or hilly, the direction in which it slopes, the drainage, streams, ponds, or lakes. It will be important to ascertain whether the forest has been visited by fire or damaged by grazing animals. Furthermore, notes should be begun and carried throughout the observations upon the animals which inhabit or frequent the forest, and their influence upon the distribution of seeds or pollen.

Is the soil swampy, moist, or dry? What is its

composition? Is it chiefly sand, clay, or rock? Is the rock limestone, granite, or quartz? Is the soil covered with a layer of fallen leaves, or has this been destroyed?

It will next be of importance to determine the trees which make up the larger members of the community. With regard to this point two kinds may be distinguished: *pure* and *mixed* forests. A pure forest shows but one kind and a mixed forest many kinds of trees. What species is most abundant? Are the trees closely crowded together so as to completely shade the ground, or are they wide apart, thus permitting light to reach the ground and the growth of many other plants? Pure forests, made up of pines, hemlocks, or beeches generally shade the ground so completely as to make it impossible for undershrubs to live. Oak, maple, and hickory forests are generally open and have much underbrush. Make a map of the forest, showing the facts in regard to the occurrence of the different kinds of trees. The trees may be evergreen, retaining the leaves throughout the winter, or these may be cast in the autumn.

Find the seedlings or young specimens of the trees, and note whether they have found a foothold in shaded or sunny places. Find a place where a tree or clump of trees has been destroyed or died, and note whether the young trees which are springing up in their places are of the same species as the dead ones. This will do much to indicate the ultimate fate of the forest. If you find that the dead trees are being replaced by the same kind, it would mean that the condition of the forest would remain unchanged; but if different ones are gaining a foothold the entire character of the forest would be changed in the course of time. If all of the dead trees are replaced by a single species, it would indicate that finally a pure forest of that species would occupy the locality if undisturbed by man.

Find the seeds and fruits of the trees and determine the manner in which they are disseminated, and their endurance of cold and drought.

If possible find isolated trees, and note the distance to which their seeds have been carried.

Do they germinate as soon as set free from the parent, or do they lie quiescent until the following season? Observe the manner of germination.

Traverse the entire margin of the forest, and note whether it is spreading or not. Do you find young seedlings outside the area occupied by the taller trees?

Note the occurrence of *shrubs* and *small bushes*. Are they found under trees or in openings or margins? In an open or mixed forest there may be a continuous layer of shrubs over the entire area, while in close woods they can find suitable conditions only in the openings. Plot the positions of the shrubs and determine the species represented.

Climbers will be found in greater or less abundance. Some of these will be attached to the trunks of the tallest trees, while others are supported by the shrubs and low bushes.

The *carpet*, or layer of plants which cling to the surface or rise only a short distance above it, will vary greatly with the manner in which the trees are associated. In close pure forests, like the hemlock, the carpet will be sparse and almost entirely lacking from the depths of the wooded area. A few low-growing species may be found in open places or clinging to exposed rocks or hillocks. In this carpet will be found mosses, ferns, liverworts, creeping and trailing vines and shrubs, and herbaceous plants which form tufts or rosettes of leaves which lie close to the surface, like the sedges, some grasses, or the saxifrages.

The loose soil is inhabited by scores of species of fungi, which send their long strands in every direction, and occasionally develop the sporophyte in the form of stalked capsules, puff-balls, or umbrella-shaped "toadstools" or "mushrooms," while the soil is teeming with bacteria, which cause the decay of the leaves. It would be most interesting to compare the carpet of a swampy portion of the forest with that of a slope or wooded hill.

240. *Relations of members of the forest.* — The relations of the members of the forest are most close and intimate. A disturbance of one is likely to influence all the others. Thus the leaves and twigs from the trees form a light layer of loose soil or humus necessary for the growth of mosses and ferns, and the freshly fallen layer covers over the members of the carpet each autumn with a blanket which protects them from the extremes of the winter. On the other hand, the destruction of the forest and the loose soil by fire, or the action of grazing animals, would result in injuries to the trees.

241. *Time of blooming.* — It needs but the most casual acquaintance with plants to know that they do not all bloom and ripen seeds at the same time of the

year. And it may be recalled that after the opening
of the growing season in spring there is a constant
succession of flowers throughout the summer. This
is not an accidental occurrence. Each species tends
to bloom and mature its seeds at a time when it may
do so to the best advantage and with the least competition. Without going into all the points involved,
it is to be seen that if all the plants which need
insects to carry their pollen were to bloom at the
same time, the supply of honey they offer could not
secure the attention of the insects to more than
a few individuals of each species. As it is, however, every species secures a share of work of the
insects in cross-pollination, since only a few species
offer honey at the same time, and the seeds are
also disseminated with less competition. If all
the crops of a farmer were to be harvested at
the same time, they could neither be cared for nor
shipped properly.

242. *Seasonal activity.* — It must not be supposed that the activity of the members of the forest
community is confined to the season in which flowers
appear. If a close examination of the community
is made in February or March, it will be found that

many of the mosses have developed the sporophytes with their conspicuous capsules while the soil is still frozen. The closely lying rosettes and evergreen leaves have taken advantage of every sunny day, and the flowering shoots will spring up into the air on the earliest approach of spring. One species, a shrub, the witch-hazel, blooms after its leaves have fallen in October and November, and ripens its seeds the next summer. Make note of the species of all parts of the forest which bloom in the early part of the spring, during a period of a month. Some kinds will be found which form flowers before the leaves are up out of the ground, or are unfolded from the buds. The first period should cover all the time until the leaves of the trees have appeared.

Make similar note of the species which bloom before the opening of summer, or June 1st. What are the earliest species to mature seeds and drop them to the ground? Do these seeds germinate at once, or lie dormant until the next year?

Keep one or two species under constant observation, and determine the length of time between the beginning of growth and the maturation of the seeds and their germination.

It will be of equally great interest to follow the activities of the forest members through early summer, midsummer, late summer, autumn, and late autumn, until the closing of the season.

243. *Families and species in the community.* — The work outlined in the previous pages should enable the student to make a census of the families and species which make up the community. This should be done in connection with the study of the various elements in the forest. The student should provide himself with a manual of the flora of the region in which he is located, and make himself familiar with the use of it so that he can identify the majority of the species met with. The study of the forest enables one to group plants according to habit and place in the community, but the study of the flora gives a classification according to relationship and descent.

Bring together specimens of species belonging to the same genus, or family, and note their differences and similarities in appearance.

Compare individuals of the same species which live in different kinds of soil, or in more or less light. If possible, compare a swamp forest with an upland forest in all the above particulars.

244. *Meadows.* — Natural meadows will not be easy to find in the regions accessible to most readers of this book. All have been mowed, or pastured by grazing animals to such extent that the original arrangement of the various members of the community has been very much disturbed. Nothing makes this more apparent than to find a meadow that has been allowed to run to weeds. This does not mean that the meadow returns to its natural state. But, as soon as man ceases to protect the plants he wishes to cultivate and to renew them by additions of seed brought from elsewhere, they come into competition with vigorously growing species which overtop them and partially crowd them out, resulting in a new meadow. It may be seen that the chief members in a meadow are low grasses, clovers, small creepers, a few stray mosses and liverworts, and a large number of perennial herbs which form rosettes of leaves on the surface and send up tall flowering stalks, like the thistle, ironweed, mullein, joe-pye, and many others. Perhaps the most natural meadows will be offered

by the open spaces in woodlands.   Observe a spot of this character, and note whether the young trees from the forest are taking possession or not.

245. *Rock societies.* — Find a set of cliffs or exposed ridge of rocks, and note the character of the vegetation that finds a foothold there.   It will be seen that the distribution of the rock plants is limited quite exactly by the extent of the stone on which they grow.   This is perhaps the most striking feature about these communities.   Forests may cover many square miles in extent, but rock societies usually extend over a few square yards only.   Still another feature will be brought out in a comparison of the rock society and the forest; the thousands of individuals in the forest crowd each other fiercely for space in which to live, while the members of the rock societies are scattered about over the hard surface, finding a foothold where they may in any convenient crevice or roughened area   Observe a rock society throughout a portion of the season, and make a census of its members.   The number of seed plants will be small.   Ferns will probably be represented, the mosses will form clumps or coatings on moist portions of the rock, some liverworts

will be present; but the plant most at home in such places is a flat-crusted one, of various shades of greenish-brown, which lies flat on the surface, growing vigorously in the wet seasons, and shrinking to a hard brittle mass in dry weather. These are the lichens, and other members of this group sheathe the trunks of trees in the forest. Compare the species found on different slopes of the rock.

246. *Pond societies.* — Pond societies live in almost all waters except those of lakes and streams polluted by the sewage of cities. The constitution of such societies may be best studied in a pond, lake, or sluggish stream, and a boat will be a useful adjunct for the exploration of depths which cannot be reached by wading. The soil above high water will be very moist, offering suitable conditions for a belt of cat-tails, then one of flowering plants, willows, and small shrubs, and back of these the trees of a forest.

On the first visit to the place chosen for study, note the extreme height to which the water rises, and examine first the plants growing between the high-water mark and the edge of the water. Identify

them, and note their habits of growth and reproduction.   How are their seeds disseminated ?

Two main classes of plants will be found in the
water : one, which anchors to the bottom, entirely
submerged or partly floating, and another which
floats freely on the surface.   In the first class will
be found many algæ, which coat the stones at the
bottom of the shallow places, and pond-weeds, water-
lilies, arrow-leaf.   Determine the form in which
these species live through the winter.   Observe
the action of the flower stalk of the water arum.
How are the seeds of these plants spread from place
to place ?

One of the members of this group, Vallisneria, lives
entirely underneath the surface, sending its pistillate
flowers up to the surface, at the end of long stalks,
while those containing stamens only, break off and
float.   After the pistils have received the pollen,
the maturing seed-pods are drawn down under the
water by the action of the stalk, which assumes the
form of a corkscrew.   Similar action is exhibited by
the water hyacinth, which roots in the mud in
shallow water or floats about in colonies.   When
the seeds are formed, the stalks bend over, thrusting
the pods under the water.

Note the species floating on the surface. Among these may be found the minute duckweeds, which look like small leaves, and are of such size that several of them may be laid side by side on the thumb nail. The leaflike body represents both leaves and stems, while but one slender root is present that trails down in the water and serves as a keel to prevent the upsetting of the leaf (§ 31). A vivid coloring may be seen on the lower side of these and other floating aquatic organs. In places the surface may be taken up by numerous specimens of the bladderwort with their curiously pouched leaves full of minute entrapped animals. In quiet pools, free from the action of currents, the surface will be covered by heavy masses of a greenish scum, which has a greasy feel when held between the fingers. This is a very widely distributed alga, Spirogyra, and the masses are composed of long threads made up of cylindrical cells placed end to end. What becomes of all these floating members of the community in the winter time? How do they reappear in the spring?

247. *Locations occupied by members of different kinds of communities.* — Low-lying areas may be

P

found in land which is not well drained that support groups of members from two different kinds of communities. This is to be seen in places covered with water by the spring floods, which last until early summer. During this time the only species living in the place are aquatic, both floating and rooting. With the advance of summer the water evaporates, leaving the soil dry and suitable for some of the rapidly growing members of swamp or meadow societies. A few species of algæ, as well as some of the seed plants, are so elastic in their habits that they grow under both conditions. Thus the alga, green velt (Vaucheria), may float or rest on moist soil with equal facility. Species which cannot adapt themselves in this manner live through the unfavorable period in the form of seeds, tubers, or corms. The continuation of either the floods by artificial or natural dams, or the complete drainage of the area, will result in the extinction of the members of the group least adapted to withstand the change.

248. *Extermination of a forest.* — Find a piece of woodland from which the trees have been recently cut, and note the changes ensuing among the other members of the community.

249. *Fields.* — Examine a cultivated field, and note the kinds or species which exist there with the crop plants. Do they belong to meadows, forests, or swamps?

250. *Course of further study.* — The work followed in this book will give a general idea of the mode of life and purposes of the plant world. It will next be in order for the student to examine the structure and development of representative types of the great groups in which plants are divided, — algæ, fungi, liverworts, mosses, ferns, and seed plants, — in order to comprehend their descent and relationship, and the general laws by which plants adapt their bodies to their environment.

INDEX

LESSONS WITH PLANTS

Suggestions for Seeing and Interpreting Some of the Common
Forms of Vegetation

By L. H. BAILEY
Professor of Horticulture in the Cornell University

With Delineations from Nature by W. S. HOLDSWORTH, of the
University of Michigan

523 pages. 446 illustrations. 12mo. Cloth. $1.10, net

There are two ways of looking at nature   The *old way*, which you have
found so unsatisfactory, was to classify everything — to consider leaves, roots,
and whole plants as formal herbarium specimens, forgetting that each had its
own story of growth and development, struggle and success, to tell.   Nothing
stifles a natural love for plants more effectually than that old way.

The new way is to watch the life of every growing thing, to look upon each
plant as a living creature, whose life is a story as fascinating as the story of any
favorite hero   "Lessons with Plants" is a book of stories, or rather a book
of plays, for we can see each chapter acted out, if we take the trouble to *look*
at the actors.   It is a book, too, that enables any one to read Nature's stories
for himself.

Darwin L. Bardwell, Superintendent of Schools, Binghamton.
> "I have spent some time in most delightful examination of it, and the
> longer I look, the better I like it.   I find it not only full of interest, but emi-
> nently suggestive.   I know of no book which begins to do so much to open
> the eyes of the student — whether pupil or teacher — to the wealth of meaning
> contained in simple plant forms.   Above all else it seems to be full of sugges-
> tions that help one to learn the language of plants, so they may talk to him."

Professor V. M Spalding, University of Michigan.
> " It is an admirable book, and cannot fail both to awaken interest in the
> subject, and to serve as a helpful and reliable guide to young students of
> plant life.   It will, I think, fill an important place in secondary schools, and
> comes at an opportune time when helps of this kind are needed and eagerly
> sought."

THE MACMILLAN COMPANY

NEW YORK   BOSTON   CHICAGO   SAN FRANCISCO

CPSIA information can be obtained
at www.ICGtesting.com
Printed in the USA
LVHW110325241221
707119LV00008B/140